BY BRENÉ BROWN

BRAVING THE WILDERNESS

BRAVING THE WILDERNESS

The Quest for True Belonging
and the Courage to Stand Alone

BRENÉ BROWN, PHD, LMSW

RANDOM HOUSE | NEW YORK

2019 Random House Trade Paperback Edition

Published in the United States by Random House,
an imprint and division of Penguin Random House LLC, New York.

RANDOM HOUSE and the HOUSE colophon are registered trademarks of
Penguin Random House LLC.

Originally published in hardcover in the United States by
Random House, an imprint and division of
Penguin Random House LLC, in 2017.

LIBRARY OF CONGRESS CATALOGING-IN-PUBLICATION DATA
Names: Brown, Brené, author.
Title: Braving the wilderness : the quest for true belonging and
the courage to stand alone / Brené Brown, PhD, LMSW.
Description: New York : Random House, [2017] |
Includes bibliographical references and index.
Identifiers: LCCN 2017030221 | ISBN 9780812985818 (paperback) |
ISBN 9780525508694 (international edition) |
ISBN 9780812995855 (ebook)
Subjects: LCSH: Group identity. | Courage. | Individuality.
Classification: LCC HM753.B765 2017 | DDC 305.8—dc23 LC
record available at https://lccn.loc.gov/2017020221

Printed in the United States of America on acid-free paper

randomhousebooks.com

4 6 8 9 7 5 3

Title-page art: Borchee/iStock by Getty Images
Chapter-opening art: kovalto1/Shutterstock.com

*To my father: Thank you for insisting that
I always speak up and take a stand—
even when you passionately disagree*

CONTENTS
• • •

BRAVING THE WILDERNESS

ONE

Everywhere and Nowhere

When I start writing, I inevitably feel myself swallowed by fear. And it's especially true when I notice that findings from my research are going to challenge long-held beliefs or ideas. When this happens, it doesn't take long before I start thinking, *Who am I to say this?* Or, *I'm really going to piss people off if I call their ideas into question.*

In these uncertain and risky moments of vulnerability, I search for inspiration from the brave innovators and disrupters whose courage feels contagious. I read and watch everything by them or about them that I can get my hands on—every interview, every essay, every lecture, every book. I do this so that when I need them, when I'm living in my fear, they come to sit with me and cheer me on. Most important, while watching over my shoulder, they put up with very little of my bullshit.

Developing this process took time. In my earlier years, I tried the opposite approach—filling my mind with critics and naysayers. I would sit at my desk and picture the faces of my least favorite professors, my harshest and most cynical colleagues, and my most unforgiving online critics. *If I can keep them happy*, I thought, *or at the very least quiet, I'll be good to go.* The outcome was the worst-case scenario for a researcher or a social scientist: findings that were gently folded into a preexisting way of seeing the world; findings that carefully nudged existing ideas but did so without upsetting anyone; findings that were safe, filtered, and comfortable. But none of that was authentic. It was a tribute.

So I decided that I had to fire those naysayers and fearmongers. In their places, I began to summon up men and women who have shaped the world with their courage and creativity. And who have, at least on occasion, pissed people off. They are a varied bunch. J. K. Rowling, author of the Harry Potter books I love so much, is my go-to person when I'm struggling with how to introduce a new and strange world of ideas that has only just emerged from my research. I imagine her telling me: *New worlds are important, but you can't just describe them. Give us the stories that make up that universe. No matter how wild and weird the new world might be, we'll see ourselves in the stories.*

The author and activist bell hooks comes to the fore when there's a painful conversation happening around race, gender, or class. She's taught me about teaching as a sacred act and the importance of discomfort in learning. And Ed Catmull, Shonda Rhimes, and Ken Burns stand behind me, whispering in my ear, while I'm telling a story. They nudge me when I become impatient and start skipping the details and dialogue that bring meaning to storytelling. "Take us with you into that story," they insist. Countless musicians and artists also show up, as does Oprah. Her advice is tacked to the wall in my study: "Do not think you can be brave with your life and your work and never disappoint anyone. It doesn't work that way."

But my oldest and most steadfast counselor is Maya Angelou. I was introduced to her work thirty-two years ago when I was studying poetry in college. I read her poem "Still I Rise" and everything shifted for me. It contained such power and beauty. I collected every Angelou book, poem, and interview I could find, and her words taught me, pushed me, and healed me. She managed to be both full of joy *and* unsparing.

But there was one quote from Maya Angelou that I deeply disagreed with. It was a quote on belonging, which I came across when I was teaching a course on race and class at the University of Houston. In an interview with Bill Moyers that aired on public television in 1973, Dr. Angelou said:

> You are only free when you realize you belong no place—you belong every place—no place at all. The price is high. The reward is great.

I can remember exactly what I thought when I read that quote. *That's just wrong. What kind of world would it be if we*

*belonged nowhere? Just a bunch of lonely people coexisting. I don't
think she understands the power of belonging.*

For over twenty years, whenever that quote popped up
in my life, I felt a rush of anger. *Why would she say that?
That's not true. Belonging is essential. We must belong to something, to someone, to somewhere.* I soon realized that the anger
came from two places. First, Dr. Angelou had come to
mean so much to me that I just couldn't stand the thought
that we disagreed on something so fundamental. Second,
the need to fit in and the ache of not belonging was one
of the most painful threads in my own life. I couldn't accept
the idea of "belonging nowhere" as freedom. Feeling like I
never truly belonged anywhere was my greatest pain, a personal suffering that threaded through most of my pre-adult
life.

It was in no way my liberation.

Experiences of not belonging are the time markers of
my life, and they started early. I attended pre-K and kindergarten at Paul Habans Elementary on the west bank of
New Orleans. It was 1969, and as wonderful as the city was
and still is, it was a place suffocated by racism. Schools had
only become officially desegregated the year I started. I
didn't know or understand much about what was happening, I was too young; but I knew that my mom was outspo-
ken and tenacious. She spoke up a lot and even wrote a
letter to the *Times-Picayune* challenging the legality of what
today we'd call racial profiling. I could sense that energy
around her, but to me, she was still just a volunteer in my

homeroom and the person who made me, herself, and my Barbie matching yellow plaid shift dresses.

We had moved there from Texas, and that had been hard for me. I desperately missed my grandmother, but I was eager to make new friends at school and around our apartment complex. It quickly got complicated, though. Homeroom lists were used to determine *everything*—from attendance records to birthday party invitations. One day my mom's room-mother partner waved the list in front of my mom's face and said, "Look at all of the black kids on here! Look at these names! *They're all named Casandra!*"

Huh, my mom thought. Maybe this explained why I was being left out of so many of my white friends' parties. My mom goes by her middle name, but her first name is Casandra. My full name on that homeroom list? Casandra Brené Brown. If you're African American and reading this, you know exactly why white families weren't inviting me over. It's the same reason a group of African American graduate students gave me a card at the end of the semester that said, "OK. You really are Brené Brown." They had signed up for my course on women's issues and almost fell out of their chairs when I walked to my desk at the front of the classroom on the first day of class. One student said, "You are *not* Casandra Brené Brown?" *Yes, ma'am*. It's also why, when I walked into a job interview for a part-time receptionist at a doctor's office in San Antonio, the woman said, "*You're* Brené Brown! Well, what a pleasant surprise!" And yes, I walked out of the interview before we sat down.

The black families were welcoming to me—but their shock was noticeable when I walked through the door. One of my friends told me I was the first white person who had ever been inside their house. That's hard to wrap your head around when you're four years old and you're really there for pin-the-tail-on-the-donkey and to eat cake with your friends. As simple as belonging should be in kindergarten, I was already struggling to understand why I felt on the outside of every group.

The next year we moved to the Garden District so my dad could be closer to Loyola, and I transferred into Holy Name of Jesus. I was an Episcopalian, which made me one of the only non-Catholic students in my school. Turned out I was the wrong religion, yet another wedge between me and belonging. After a year or two of sitting out, being called out, and sometimes being left out, I was sent to the office, and arrived to find God waiting for me. At least that's who I thought it was. It turned out to be a bishop. He handed me a mimeographed copy of the Nicene Creed and we went through it, line by line. When we were done, he handed me a note to take home to my parents. The note read, "Brené is Catholic now."

Still, things were relatively good for the next couple of years as I started to get into the groove of my new life in New Orleans, mostly because I had the best BFF in the world—Eleanor. But then came a bunch of big moves. We left New Orleans for Houston when I was in fourth grade. Then we left Houston for Washington, D.C., when I was in sixth grade. Then we left Washington when I was in eighth grade and moved back to Houston. The normal turbulence and awkwardness of middle school was magnified by perpetual "new-girl-ness." My only saving grace was that during all of these transitions, my parents were in a good place and getting along. This meant that despite the turbulence around me with ever-changing schools, friends, and adults, home was safe. It even felt like a refuge from the pain of not belonging. When all else failed, I belonged at home, with my family.

But things started to break. That last move back to Houston was the beginning of the long, miserable end to my parents' marriage. And right on top of that chaos, there were the Bearkadettes.

When we moved back to Houston at the very end of eighth grade there was, thankfully, just enough time to try out for the high school drill team, called the Bearkadettes. This was to be my everything. In a house that was increasingly filled with the muffled sounds of my parents arguing, heard through the walls of my bedroom, that drill team was salvation. Just picture it: lines of girls in white-fringed blue satin vests and short skirts, all of them wearing uniform wigs, white cowboy boots, small white cowboy hats, and bright red lipstick, strutting into high school football stadiums filled with crowds afraid to leave their seats during halftime lest they miss the high kicks and perfectly choreographed routines. This was my way out, my new, pretty, impeccably ordered refuge.

Eight years of ballet was plenty to get me through the task of learning the routine, and a two-week liquid diet got me through the brutal weigh-in. All of the girls swore by the cabbage soup and water diet. It's hard to think of letting a twelve-year-old go on a liquid diet, but for some reason it seemed normal.

To this day, I'm not sure I've ever wanted anything in my life more than I wanted a place on this drill team. The perfection, precision, and beauty of it would not only offset the growing turmoil at home, but also deliver the holy grail of belonging. I would have a "big sis" and she would decorate my locker. We'd have sleepovers and date football players. For a kid who had seen *Grease* forty-five times, I knew this was the beginning of a high school experience that included sudden, spontaneous sing-alongs and the 1980s version of sock hops.

And most of all, I would be a part of something that literally did everything together in lockstep. A Bearkadette was belonging personified.

I didn't really have any friends yet, so I was on my own for tryouts. The routine was easy to learn—a jazzy number performed to a big band version of "Swanee" (you know, the "how I love ya, how I love ya" one). There was a lot of sliding with jazz hands and an entire section of high kicks. I could kick higher than all of the girls except one dancer named LeeAnne. I practiced so much that I could do that routine in my sleep. I still remember parts of it today.

Tryout day was terrifying, and I'm not sure if it was my nerves or the starvation diet, but I was lightheaded when I woke up, and I stayed that way after my mom dropped me off at the school. Now, as the mother of a teen and a tween, it's a little hard to think of how I had to walk in by myself, surrounded by groups of girls who were piling out of cars and running in together, holding hands. But I soon realized I had a bigger problem than walking in alone.

All of the girls—and I mean *all* of the girls—were made up from head to toe. Some were wearing blue satin shorts and gold shirts, and others had blue and gold tank tops with little white skirts. There was every iteration of blue and gold bows that you could imagine. And they were all in full makeup. I had on no makeup, and I was wearing gray cotton shorts over a black leotard. No one had told me that you were supposed to get decked out in school colors. Everyone looked so bright and shiny. I looked like the sad girl whose parents fight a lot.

I made the weigh-in with six pounds to spare. Even so, the sight of girls stepping off the scale and running into the locker room weeping traumatized me.

We wore numbers safety-pinned to our shirts and danced in groups of five or six. Lightheaded or not, I nailed the routine. I felt pretty confident when my mom picked me up and I went home to wait it out. They would post the numbers later that evening. Those hours in between moved in slow motion.

Finally, at five after six, we pulled in to the parking lot of my soon-to-be high school. My entire family—mom, dad, brother and sisters—was in the car. I was going to check my number and then we were headed to San Antonio to visit my grandparents. I walked up to the poster board hanging on the outside of the gym door. Standing next to me was one of the girls from my tryout group. She was the brightest and shiniest of all the girls. And on top of all that, her name was Kris. Yes, she even had one of those coveted girl-boy names that we all wanted.

The list was in numeric order. If your number was there, you'd made the team. If your number wasn't there, you were out. I was number 62. My eye went straight for the 60s: 59, 61, 64, 65. I looked again. I just couldn't process it. I thought if I stared hard enough and the universe knew how much was on the line, the number might magically appear. I was ripped out of my negotiation with the universe by Kris's screaming. She was jumping up and down, and before I could make sense of what was happening, her dad had jumped out of the car, run up to her, grabbed her, and twirled her around, just like in the movies. I would later hear through the grapevine that I was a solid dancer but not really Bearkadette material. No bows. No shine. No group. No friends. Nowhere to belong.

I was alone. And it felt devastating.

I walked back to our station wagon and got in the backseat, and my dad drove away. My parents didn't say one word. Not a single word. The silence cut into me like a knife to the heart. They were ashamed of me and for me. My dad had been captain of the football team. My mom had been head of her drill team. I was nothing. My parents, especially my father, valued being cool and fitting in above all else. I was not cool. I didn't fit in.

And now, for the first time, I didn't belong to my family either.

My drill team story is one that's easy to dismiss as un-important in the larger scheme of what's going on in the world today. (I can already see the #firstworldproblems hashtag.) But let me tell you what it meant to me. I don't know if this was true or it was the story I told myself in that silence, but that became the day I no longer belonged in my family—the most primal and important of all of our social groups. Had my parents consoled me or told me I was brave for trying—or, better yet and what I really wanted in that moment, had they taken my side and told me how terrible it was and how I deserved to be picked—this story wouldn't be one that defined my life and shaped its trajectory. But it did.

Sharing this story was so much more difficult than I thought it would be. I had to go to iTunes to remember the name of the tryout song, and when I played the preview, I just started sobbing. I didn't break down because I hadn't made the drill team, I wept for the girl that I couldn't com-fort back then. The girl who didn't understand what was happening or why. I wept for the parents who were so ill equipped to deal with my pain and vulnerability. Parents who just didn't have the skills to speak up and comfort me or, at the very least, run an interception on the story of not belonging with them or to them. These are the moments that, when left unspoken and unresolved, send us into our adult lives searching desperately for belonging and settling for fitting in. Luckily, my parents never harbored the illusion that parenting ends when your kids leave the house. We've learned about courage, vulnerability, and true belonging together. That's been the little miracle.

Even in the context of suffering—poverty, violence, human rights violations—not belonging in our families is still one of the most dangerous hurts. That's because it has the power to break our heart, our spirit, and our sense of self-worth. It broke all three for me. And when those things break, there are only three outcomes, something I've borne witness to in my life and in my work:

1. You live in constant pain and seek relief by numbing it and/or inflicting it on others;

2. You deny your pain, and your denial ensures that you pass it on to those around you and down to your children; or

3. You find the courage to own the pain and develop a level of empathy and compassion for yourself and others that allows you to spot hurt in the world in a unique way.

I certainly tried the first two. Only through sheer grace did I make my way to the third.

After the Bearkadette nightmare, the fighting got worse at home. They were often no-holds-barred battles. My parents just didn't have the skills to do it another way. Telling myself that my parents were the only ones in the world who were struggling to keep a marriage together, I felt tremendous shame. All of the friends of my brother and sisters who played at our house called my parents "Mr. and Mrs. B" with a casual cool, like they were great. But I knew about the secret fighting and knew I didn't belong with those friends whose parents were as awesome as the ones on TV. So now the shame of secrecy was piling in, too.

Of course, perspective is a function of experience. I didn't have the experience to put what was happening around me in context, and my parents were just trying to survive without inflicting catastrophic damage, so I don't think it dawned on them to share their perspectives with us. I was *certain* that I was the only one in town, even in the world, living through this specific kind of shit show, despite the fact that my high school was in the national news for the alarming number of students there who had committed suicide. It was only later, once the world changed and people started to actually talk about their struggles, that I found out how many of those perfect parents ended up divorced, dead from hard living, or, mercifully, in recovery.

Sometimes the most dangerous thing for kids is the silence that allows them to construct their own stories—stories that almost always cast them as alone and unworthy of love and belonging. That was my narrative, so rather than doing high kicks during halftime, I was the girl hiding weed in her beanbag chair and running with the wild kids, looking for my people any way I could. I never tried out for a single thing again. Instead, I got really good at fitting in by doing whatever it took to feel like I was wanted and a part of something.

During my parents' ongoing and worsening fights, my

brother and two sisters would usually come into my room to wait it out. As the oldest, I started using my newly formed fitting-in superpowers to identify what had led to the fighting, so I could concoct elaborate interventions to "make things better." I could be the savior for my siblings, for my family. When it worked, I considered myself a hero. When it didn't, I'd blame myself and double down on the data finding. It's only just dawning on me as I write this—this is actually when I started choosing research and data over vulnerability.

As I look back, I realize I probably owe my career to not belonging. First as a child, then as a teenager, I found my primary coping mechanism for not belonging in studying people. I was a seeker of pattern and connection. I knew if I could recognize patterns in people's behaviors and connect those patterns to what people were feeling and doing, I could find my way. I used my pattern recognition skills to anticipate what people wanted, what they thought, or what they were doing. I learned how to say the right thing or show up in the right way. I became an expert fitter-in, a chameleon. And a very lonely stranger to myself.

As time passed, I grew to know many of the people around me better than they knew themselves, but in that process, I lost me. By the time I was twenty-one years old, I had dropped in and out of college, survived my parents' divorce, hitchhiked through Europe for six months, and engaged in every self-destructive, dumb-ass behavior you can name, short of hard drugs. But I was growing weary. I was running on fumes. Anne Lamott quoted an observation from one of her sober friends that sums up that kind of running away perfectly: "By the end I was deteriorating faster than I could lower my standards."

In 1987, I met Steve. For some reason, I was more myself with him than I had been with anyone since my first BFF, Eleanor. He saw me. And even though he caught the tail end of my self-destructive days, he saw the real me and he liked me. He came from very similar family trauma, so he recognized the hurt, and for the first time in both of our lives, we talked about our experiences. We cracked open. We would sometimes talk for ten hours over the phone. We talked about every fight we witnessed, the loneliness we battled, and the unbearable pain of not belonging.

What started as a friendship turned into a huge crush, then a total love affair. Never underestimate the power of being seen—it's exhausting to keep working against yourself when someone truly sees you and loves you. Some days his love felt like a gift. Other days I hated his guts for it. But as I started to catch glimpses of my true self, I was filled with grief and longing. Grief for the girl who never belonged anywhere and a longing to figure out who I was, what I liked, what I believed in, and where I wanted to go. Steve wasn't threatened at all by my soul-searching. He loved it. He supported it.

So no, Dr. Angelou, belonging nowhere couldn't be a *good* thing. I still didn't understand what she meant.

Seven years after we met, Steve and I got married. He went from medical school to residency, and I went from undergrad to grad school. In 1996, the day after I finished my master's, I decided to make my clean living commitment official and quit drinking and smoking. Interestingly, my first temporary AA sponsor told me, "I don't think you *belong* in AA. You should try the codependents' meetings." The codependency sponsor told me to go back to AA or try OA, since "you're not exactly one of us." Can you believe it? What kind of shit is it when you don't even belong at AA?

Finally, a new sponsor told me I had the pu-pu platter of addictions: Basically, I used whatever I could find to not feel vulnerable. She told me to find a meeting that spoke to me—it didn't matter which one as long as I stopped drinking, smoking, caretaking, and overeating. *Sure. Gotcha.*

Those early years of marriage were tough. We were broke and mentally strung out from residency and grad school. I'll never forget telling a school therapist that I just didn't think it was going to work out. Her response? "It may not. He likes you way more than you like you."

My journey from expert-level fitting in to true belonging started in my early twenties and took a couple of decades. Through my thirties, I traded one type of self-destruction for another: I gave up partying for perfectionism. I still wrestled with being an outsider—even in my work—but what changed was my response to not seeing my number on the poster board. Rather than suffering in silence and shame, I started to talk about my fears and my hurt. I started questioning what was important to me and why. Was living in lockstep really how I wanted to spend my life? No. When I was told I couldn't do a qualitative dissertation, I did it anyway. When they tried to convince me not to study shame, I did it anyway. When they told me I couldn't be a professor and write books that people might actually want to read, I did it anyway.

It wasn't that I swung from one extreme—finding value only in fitting in—to another—finding value only in being different, defiant, or contrarian. Those are two sides of the same coin. I was actually still craving belonging, and my decisions to be on the outside of my profession kept me in almost constant anxiety and scarcity. It wasn't ideal, but I had come far enough to know that the price of assimilating and doing what was expected of me would have cost me too much—possibly my health, my marriage, or my sobriety. As much as I wanted a crew, I'd stay on the outside before I sacrificed any of those.

Then, in 2013, a series of little miracles happened that led to one of the most important moments of my life. Oprah Winfrey invited me to be a guest on one of my favorite shows, *Super Soul Sunday*.

The night before the show, I went out to eat with one of the producers and my manager, Murdoch (a Scotsman who lives in the West Village and who now says *y'all* as easily as I do). After dinner, as Murdoch and I were walking back to the hotel, he stopped on the corner and called to me as I kept walking, "Where are you, Brené?"

When I gave him a smart-ass answer—"On the corner of Michigan and Chicago"—I knew I was feeling vulnerable. And as Murdoch proceeded to explain how "not present" I was at dinner—Polite and friendly? *Yes.* Present? *No.*—I knew right away what was happening. I looked at

Murdoch and admitted, "I'm doing that thing I do when I'm afraid. I'm floating above my life, watching it and studying it, rather than living it."

Murdoch nodded. "I know. But you need to find a way to stop and bring yourself back here. This is a big deal. I don't want you to miss it. Don't study this moment. Be in it."

The next morning, as I was getting dressed to meet Oprah for the first time, my daughter texted me. She wanted to make sure I had signed and returned a permission slip for her school trip. After assuring her that I had, I sat on the edge of my bed and fought back tears. I started thinking, *I need a permission slip to stop being so serious and afraid. I need permission to have fun today.* That got the idea started. After I looked around my room to make sure no one was watching the incredibly ridiculous thing I was about to do, I walked over to the desk in my room, sat down, and wrote myself a permission slip on a Post-it note from my computer bag. It simply said, "Permission to be excited and goofy and to have fun."

It would be the first of hundreds of permission slips I would go on to write for myself. I still write them today and I teach everyone who will give me five minutes of their time the power of this intention-setting method. It totally works. But as with the permission slips you give your kids, they may have permission to go to the zoo, but they still need to get on the bus. Set the intention. Follow through. That day, I got on the bus.

I didn't realize it then, but looking back, those permission slips to myself were actually an attempt to *belong to myself* and to no one else.

Oprah and I had our emotional first meeting on camera, and within minutes we were cutting up and laughing. She was everything I thought she'd be. Fierce and kind. Gentle and tough. The hour went by in a flash. When our time was up, Oprah turned to me and said, "We should do another hour—another episode." I looked around uneasily, like we might get in trouble for even thinking this.

"Really?" I asked. "Are you sure?"

Oprah smiled. "Really. We have a lot more to talk about."

I squinted into the darkness of the studio toward what I assumed was some kind of control room and said, "Do you think we should ask?"

Oprah smiled again. "Who do you think we should run it by?" She didn't say this in an arrogant way. I think she thought my question was funny.

"Oh, right. Sorry. Then, yes. *Yes!* I'd love it! But shouldn't I change clothes? Oh, shit. I only have this outfit and the jeans and cowboy boots I wore here."

"Boots and jeans are great. I'll lend you a top."

She walked away to change her own clothes, but before she took more than a few steps, she turned back and said, "Maya Angelou is here. Would you like to meet her?"

Tunnel vision. Time slowed down. *It's all too much. Maybe I'm dead.*

"Brené? Hello? Would you like to meet Dr. Maya?" I was thinking that this really might push me over the edge when Oprah asked again, "Interested?"

I jumped out of my seat. "Yes. Oh, my God! *Yes.*"

Oprah took my hand as we walked to a second green room across the hall from the one where I got ready for the show. We went in, and the first thing I noticed was a TV screen across from where Dr. Angelou was sitting. The image on the screen showed the two empty chairs where Oprah and I had been sitting.

Maya Angelou looked straight at me. "Hello, Dr. Brown. I've been watching you."

I walked up and took her extended hand and said, "It's such an honor to meet you. You've meant so much to me. You're such a big part of my life."

She kept holding my hand and placed her other hand on top of mine. "You're doing important work. Keep doing it. Keep talking about your work. Don't stop and don't let anyone get in your way."

Then I told her that sometimes, when I teach, I turn the lights out and play for the class an old cassette tape I have of her reciting her poem "Our Grandmothers." I told her how I would sometimes just replay that line, "I shall not be moved. . . ."

She held my hands even tighter, looked right into my eyes, and with a slow and deep voice sang, "Like a tree planted by the river, I shall not be moved." Then she squeezed my hands hard and said, "Do not be moved, Brené."

It was as if she bundled up all the courage I'll ever need in my entire life and handed it to me. Rarely do you have the gift of knowing you're inside a moment that will be part of what defines you. But I knew. What do you do when you've spent the majority of your life moving to try to fit in, and all of a sudden Maya Angelou is singing to you and telling you not to be moved? You learn how to plant your damn feet is what you do. You bend and stretch and grow, but you commit to not moving from who you are. Or, at the very least, you start trying.

Six months after that unbelievable day, I found myself sitting in another green room in Chicago. This time I was speaking at one of the largest leadership events in the world. The event organizers had *strongly* recommended that I wear "business attire" to the event, and I was staring down at my black slacks and pumps and feeling like an imposter. Or like I was going to a funeral.

I was sitting with another speaker (a woman who would eventually become a good friend), and she asked how I was doing. I confessed that I was coming out of my skin and that I couldn't shake the feeling of playing dress-up. She told me I looked "really nice," but the expression on her face said, *I know. It's hard. But what can we do?*

I abruptly stood up, grabbed my suitcase from a wall lined with suitcases belonging to the other speakers, and went to the restroom. Minutes later, I came out in a navy shirt, dark jeans, and clogs. The woman looked at me, smiled, and said, "Awesome. You're brave."

I wasn't sure if she meant it or not, but I laughed. "Not

really. It's a necessity. I can't go on that stage and talk about authenticity and courage when I don't feel authentic or brave. I physically can't do it. I'm not here so my business self can talk to their business selves. I'm here to talk from my heart to their hearts. This is who I am." Another important step in learning to belong to myself.

I collided with the business world again a couple of weeks later. While going through a stack of information on upcoming speaking events, I read a note from one organizer: "We heard you speak at a conference last year. We can't wait to have you speak to our leaders! When we saw you, you talked about the importance of knowing your core values—we love that. However, you mentioned faith as one of your two guiding values. Given the business context, we'd appreciate you not mentioning faith. Courage was the other one of your values and that's great. Can you stick to that one?"

I could feel my chest tightening and my face growing hotter by the second. Something similar, though at the other extreme, had happened earlier that year. An event organizer had told me that while he "appreciated my direct and down-home approach," he'd like me to not curse, which risked losing some of the "faithful audience" who would "offer me grace" but still be offended.

Bull. Shit. This is total bullshit. I'm not doing this. I'd rather never speak again. I am done moving.

I've spent my entire career sitting across from people, listening to them tell me about the hardest and most painful moments of their lives. After fifteen years of this work,

I can confidently say that stories of pain and courage almost always include two things: *praying and cussing*. Sometimes at the exact same time.

I grabbed my sneakers, put them on, and headed out the front door to think about my response as I marched through my neighborhood. By the time I rounded the last corner before my house, I had settled on what I would say to any and all requests like these: If you think I'm going to clean up the truth or put a spit-shine on people's honest experiences, you're wrong. I'm not going to go all Joe Pesci in *Goodfellas*, but if you can't handle me saying "pissed off" or "bullshit," or you need me to pretend that faith doesn't matter to me, I'm not your girl. There are lots of great teachers and speakers—you'll just need to find one who will dress up, clean up, and shut up. That's not me. Not anymore.

I shall not be moved.

When Steve got home, I told him about my latest resolve, then sat down next to him and put my head on his shoulder. "It's hard," I said. "I don't belong anywhere. I belong no place. Everywhere I go now, I'm an outsider breaking the rules and talking about things that no one else is talking about. I've got no crew. And it's been this way my whole life."

Steve didn't try to buck me up. Instead he agreed and told me that I "kinda didn't belong" to any one group. He also reminded me that I belonged with him and Ellen and Charlie—and that I could pray and cuss all I wanted provided I had enough money to pay Charlie for the swear words.

I laughed a little, but felt tears coming on. "I've lived my entire life on the outside," I said to Steve. "It's so hard. Sometimes our house is the only place I don't feel totally alone. I don't feel I'm on a path that I understand—I can't find anyone else on it. There's no one ahead of me saying, 'It's okay. There are a lot of professor-researcher-storyteller-leadership-entrepreneur-faithful-cussers out here. Here's the blueprint.'"

Steve took my hand and said, "I know it's hard. And you must feel alone. You're kind of weird—an outlier in a lot of ways. But here's the thing: There were more than twenty speakers at that big leadership conference, and you were the highest-rated speaker. In your jeans and clogs. Given that, how do you figure that anyone belongs there more than you? You will always belong anywhere you show up as yourself and talk about yourself and your work in a real way."

And that was it. That was the moment.

I finally understood on a practical and fundamental level what Maya Angelou had said. I kissed Steve, ran into the study, grabbed my laptop, and Googled her quote. Carrying my laptop back to the couch, I read it to Steve:

You are only free when you realize you belong no place—you belong every place—no place at all. The price is high. The reward is great.

This was the moment when the core, defining story of how I saw myself—a young, lonely, not-shiny girl standing hopelessly in front of a gym door scouring a poster for confirmation that she belonged somewhere—shifted. I had achieved success with my work. I had a great partner and great kids. But until that moment, I wasn't free of that story of not belonging in my world or my family of origin.

Steve knew something was shifting. "The price *is* high. But the reward is your work getting out to the world in an honest way—a way that's true to the people who have shared their lives and stories with you."

I asked him if he really understood that strange dichotomy of being alone but still belonging—of true belonging. He said, "Yes. I feel like that all the time too. It's the paradox of feeling alone but also strong. Sometimes parents will get angry because I won't prescribe antibiotics for their child. The first thing they say is, 'Every other pediatrician does it. I'll just go to someone else.' It's not easy to hear this, but I always fall back on the thought: *It's okay if I'm alone on this. That's not what I believe is best for this child. Period.*"

My wheels started turning faster. I explained to Steve that while I felt like I now understood the vulnerability and courage of standing on your own, I still couldn't shake the underlying feeling of wanting to be a part of something. I wanted "the squad." He said, "You have a squad, but it's small and not everyone in your squad is going to agree or do the same thing. But truthfully, you hate those kinds of squads anyway." I knew he was right, but still, I wanted to understand more.

I finally stood up and told him that I had to dig into

Maya's quote and into my data on belonging. His response still makes me laugh: "Oh, I know. I know how this works. Want me to pick up dinner? I'm happy to send some food down into the research rabbit hole. Last time you walked into your study to look into something that was bugging you, it took two years."

I got hold of the full transcript of that interview between Bill Moyers and Maya Angelou, and I read for the first time these final remarks:

MOYERS: Do you belong anywhere?
ANGELOU: I haven't yet.
MOYERS: Do you belong to anyone?
ANGELOU: More and more. I mean, I belong to myself. I'm very proud of that. I am very concerned about how I look at Maya. I like Maya very much. I like the humor and courage very much. And when I find myself acting in a way that isn't . . . that doesn't please me—then I have to deal with that.

I looked up from reading this exchange and thought, *Maya belongs to Maya. I belong to myself. I get it. I don't quite have it completely, but at least I'm getting it.*

This time the research rabbit hole turned out to be four years long. I went back into the old data, collected new data, and started developing a Theory of True Belonging.

I discovered that I had a lot more to learn about what it means to truly belong.

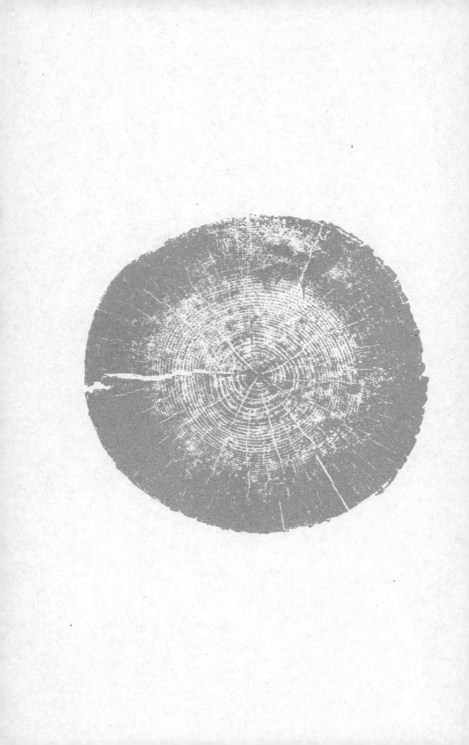

TWO

The Quest for True Belonging

True belonging.
 I don't know exactly what it is about the combination of those two words, but I do know that when I say it aloud, it just feels right. It feels like something that we all crave and need in our lives. We want to be a part of something, but we need it to be real—not conditional or fake or constantly up for negotiation. We need true belonging—but what exactly is it?

In 2010, in *The Gifts of Imperfection*, I defined belonging this way:

> Belonging is the innate human desire to be part of something larger than us. Because this yearning is so primal, we often try to acquire it by fitting in and by seeking approval, which are not only hollow substi-

tutes for belonging, but often barriers to it. Because **true belonging** only happens when we present our authentic, imperfect selves to the world, our sense of belonging can never be greater than our level of self-acceptance.

This definition has withstood the test of time as well as the emergence of new data, but it is incomplete. There's much more to true belonging. Being ourselves means sometimes having to find the courage to stand alone, totally alone. Even as I wrote this, I still thought of belonging as requiring something external to us—something we secured by, yes, showing up in a real way, but needing an experience that always involved others. So as I dug deeper into true belonging, it became clear that it's not something we achieve or accomplish with others; it's something we carry in our heart. Once we belong thoroughly to ourselves and believe thoroughly in ourselves, true belonging is ours.

Belonging to ourselves means being called to stand alone—to brave the wilderness of uncertainty, vulnerability, and criticism. And with the world feeling like a political and ideological combat zone, this is remarkably tough. We seem to have forgotten that even when we're utterly alone, we're connected to one another by something greater than group membership, politics, and ideology—that we're connected by love and the human spirit. No matter how separated we are by what we think and believe, we are part of the same spiritual story.

DEFINING TRUE BELONGING

I'm a qualitative grounded theory researcher. The goal of grounded theory is to develop theories based on people's lived experiences rather than proving or disproving existing theories. In grounded theory, researchers try to understand what we call "the main concern" of study participants. When it comes to belonging, I asked: What are people trying to achieve? What are they worried about?

The answer was surprisingly complex. They want to be a part of something—to experience real connection with others—but not at the cost of their authenticity, freedom, or power. Participants further reported feeling surrounded by "us versus them" cultures that create feelings of spiritual disconnection. When I dug deeper into what they meant by "spiritually disconnected," the research participants described a diminishing sense of shared humanity. Over and over, participants talked about their concern that the only thing that binds us together now is shared fear and disdain, not common humanity, shared trust, respect, or love. They reported feeling more afraid to disagree or debate with friends, colleagues, and family because of the lack of civility and tolerance.

Reluctant to choose between being loyal to a group and being loyal to themselves, but lacking that deeper spiritual connection to shared humanity, they were far more aware of the pressure to "fit in" and conform. Connection to a larger humanity gives people more freedom to express their individuality without fear of jeopardizing belonging. This is the spirit, which now seems missing, of saying, "Yes, we are different in many ways, but under it all we're deeply connected."

As I was defining the main concern related to belonging, I went back to *The Gifts of Imperfection* to look up the definition of spirituality that had emerged from my 2010 data:

> Spirituality is recognizing and celebrating that we are all inextricably connected to each other by a power greater than all of us, and that our connection to that power and to one another is grounded in love and compassion.

I kept reading the words "inextricably connected" over and over. We've broken that link. And in the next chapter, I'm going to show you how and why we broke it. The rest of the book is about fixing it—finding our way back to one another.

I named the main concern of participants in the current research *true belonging*. And given the definition above and the data, there was no question that a large part of the struggle for people seeking true belonging is spiritual. This is in no way a religious struggle around dogma and denominations, but is instead a wide-open, hardscrabble effort to stay connected to what binds us as humans while navigating an increasingly divisive and cynical world.

Continuing on the path of grounded theory, I focused the research on these questions:

1. What is the process, practice, or approach that the women and men who have developed a sense of true belonging have in common?

2. What does it take to get to the place in our life where we belong nowhere and everywhere—where belonging is in our heart and not a reward for "perfecting, pleasing, proving, and pretending" or something that others can hold hostage or take away?

3. If we're willing to brave the wilderness—to stand alone in our integrity—do we still need that sense of belonging that comes from community?

4. Does the current culture of increasing divisiveness affect our quest for true belonging? If so, how?

What emerged from the responses to these questions were four elements of true belonging. These elements are situated in the reality of the world we live in today. The theories that emerge from this methodology are based on how we engage with the world in our everyday lives; they're not hypothetical. This means you can't develop a theory on true belonging without addressing how our increasingly polarized world shapes our lives and our experiences of connection and true belonging. I didn't intend to write a book about belonging set against a backdrop of political and ideological chaos. But that's not my call to make. My job is to be true to the data.

As you take a look at each of the four elements, you can see that each is a daily practice and feels like a paradox. They're going to challenge us:

1. People Are Hard to Hate Close Up. Move In.
2. Speak Truth to Bullshit. Be Civil.
3. Hold Hands. With Strangers.
4. Strong Back. Soft Front. Wild Heart.

THE WILDERNESS

As a clearer picture of true belonging emerged from the data, and I realized why we must sometimes stand alone in our decisions and beliefs despite our fear of criticism and rejection, the first image that came to me was the wilderness. Theologians, writers, poets, and musicians have always used the wilderness as a metaphor, to represent everything from a vast and dangerous environment where we are forced to navigate difficult trials to a refuge of nature and beauty where we seek space for contemplation. What all wilderness metaphors have in common are the notions of solitude, vulnerability, and an emotional, spiritual, or physical quest.

Belonging so fully to yourself that you're willing to stand alone *is* a wilderness—an untamed, unpredictable place of solitude and searching. It is a place as dangerous as it is breathtaking, a place as sought after as it is feared. The wilderness can often feel unholy because we can't control it, or what people think about our choice of whether to venture into that vastness or not. But it turns out to be the place of true belonging, and it's the bravest and most sacred place you will ever stand.

The special courage it takes to experience true belonging is not just about braving the wilderness, it's about *be-*

coming the wilderness. It's about breaking down the walls, abandoning our ideological bunkers, and living from our wild heart rather than our weary hurt.

We can't expect to take a well-worn path through these badlands. While I can share what I've learned from research participants who practice true belonging in their lives, we all have to find our own way deep into the wild. And if you're like me, you're not going to like some of the terrain.

We're going to need to intentionally be with people who are different from us. We're going to have to sign up, join, and take a seat at the table. We're going to have to learn how to listen, have hard conversations, look for joy, share pain, and be more curious than defensive, all while seeking moments of togetherness.

True belonging is not passive. It's not the belonging that comes with just joining a group. It's not fitting in or pretending or selling out because it's safer. It's a practice that requires us to be vulnerable, get uncomfortable, and learn how to be present with people without sacrificing who we are. We want true belonging, but it takes tremendous courage to knowingly walk into hard moments.

BRAVING SKILLS

You don't wander into the wilderness unprepared. Standing alone in a hypercritical environment or standing together in the midst of difference requires one tool above all others: trust. To brave the wilderness and become the wilderness we must learn how to trust ourselves and trust others.

The definition of trust that best aligns with my data

comes from Charles Feltman. Feltman describes trust as "choosing to risk making something you value vulnerable to another person's actions," and he describes distrust as deciding that "what is important to me is not safe with this person in this situation (or any situation)."

Because getting our head and heart around a concept as big as trust is difficult, and because general conversations on the theme of "I don't trust you" are rarely productive, I dug into the concept to better understand what we're really talking about when we say *trust*.

Seven elements of trust emerged from the data as useful in both trusting others and trusting ourselves. I use the acronym BRAVING for the elements.

I love using BRAVING as a wilderness checklist because it reminds me that trusting myself or other people is a vulnerable and courageous process. While I shared this finding first in *Rising Strong*, I wasn't surprised to see trust emerge again in the interviews about belonging.

Trusting Others

Boundaries—You respect my boundaries, and when you're not clear about what's okay and not okay, you ask. You're willing to say no.

Reliability—You do what you say you'll do. This means staying aware of your competencies and limitations so you don't overpromise and are able to deliver on commitments and balance competing priorities.

Accountability—You own your mistakes, apologize, and make amends.

Vault—You don't share information or experiences that are not yours to share. I need to know that my confidences are kept, and that you're not sharing with me any information about other people that should be confidential.

Integrity—You choose courage over comfort. You choose what is right over what is fun, fast, or easy. And you choose to practice your values rather than simply professing them.

Nonjudgment—I can ask for what I need, and you can ask for what you need. We can talk about how we feel without judgment.

Generosity—You extend the most generous interpretation possible to the intentions, words, and actions of others.

Self-Trust

I can't imagine anything more important in the wilderness than self-trust. Fear will lead us astray and arrogance is even more dangerous. If you reread this checklist and change the pronouns, you'll see that BRAVING also works as a powerful tool for assessing our level of self-trust.

B —Did I respect my own boundaries? Was I clear about what's okay and what's not okay?

R —Was I reliable? Did I do what I said I was going to do?

A —Did I hold myself accountable?

V —Did I respect the vault and share appropriately?

I —Did I act from my integrity?

N —Did I ask for what I needed? Was I nonjudgmental about needing help?

G —Was I generous toward myself?

THE QUEST AND THE PARADOX

As I often say, I'm an experienced mapmaker, but I can be as much of a lost and stumbling traveler as anyone else. We all must find our own way. This means that, while we may be sharing the same research map, your path will be different from mine. Joseph Campbell wrote, "If you can see your path laid out in front of you step by step, you know it's not your path. Your own path you make with every step you take. That's why it's your path."

The quest for true belonging begins with this definition that I crafted from the data. It will serve as a touchstone as we move through the work together:

> **True belonging** is the spiritual practice of believing in and belonging to yourself so deeply that you can share your most authentic self with the world and find sacredness in both being a part of something and standing alone in the wilderness. True belonging doesn't require you to *change* who you are; it requires you to *be* who you are.

The only thing we know for certain is that on this quest we'll need to learn how to navigate the tension of many paradoxes along the way, including the importance of *being with* and *being alone*. In many ways, the etymology of the word "paradox" cuts right to the heart of what it means to break out of our ideological bunkers, stand on our own, and brave the wilderness. In its Greek origins, paradox is the joining of two words, *para* (contrary to) and *dokein* (opinion). The Latin *paradoxum* means "seemingly absurd but really true." True belonging is not something that you negotiate externally, it's what you carry in your heart. It's finding the sacredness in being a part of something and in braving the wilderness alone. When we reach this place, even momentarily, we belong everywhere and nowhere. *That seems absurd, but it's true.*

Carl Jung argued that a paradox is one of our most valued spiritual possessions and a great witness to the truth. It makes sense to me that we're called to combat this spiritual crisis of disconnection with one of our most valued spiritual possessions. Bearing witness to the truth is rarely easy, especially when we're alone in the wilderness.

But as Maya Angelou tells us, "The price is high. The reward is great."

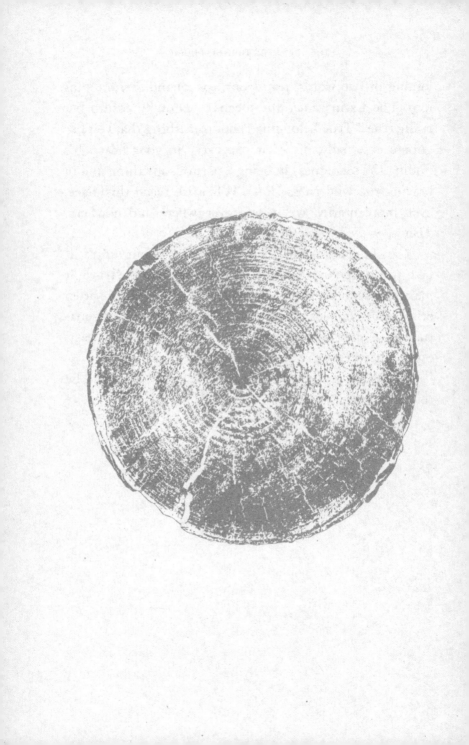

THREE

High Lonesome:
A Spiritual Crisis

S tory has it that as a child, Bill Monroe would hide in
the woods next to a railroad track in the "long, ole,
straight bottom part of Kentucky." Bill would watch World
War I veterans returning home from the war as they walked
along the track. The weary soldiers would sometimes let
out long hollers—loud, high-pitched, bone-chilling hollers
of pain and freedom that cut through the air like the blare
of a siren.

Whenever John Hartford, an acclaimed musician and
composer, tells this story, he lets out a holler of his own.
The minute you hear it, you know it. *Oh*, that *holler*. It's not
a spirited yippee or a painful wail, but—something in between. It's a holler that's thick with both misery and re-
demption. A holler that belongs to another place and time.
Bill Monroe would eventually become known as the father

of bluegrass music. During his legendary career, he often told people that he practiced that holler and "always reckoned that's where his singing style came from." Today we call that sound *high lonesome*.

High lonesome is a sound or type of music in the bluegrass tradition. Its roots go back to Bill Monroe, Roscoe Holcomb, and the bluegrass region of Kentucky. It's a kind of music I find arresting. And hard. And full of pain. When I hear Roscoe Holcomb singing "I'm a Man of Constant Sorrow," a cappella, like an arrow piercing the air, the hair on the back of my neck stands up, and I get goosebumps when I hear Bill Monroe's "I'm Blue, I'm Lonesome." When you hear that holler over the thumping mandolins and banjos, you can feel the heaviness of those soldiers' hollers, and you can even faintly make out the sound of a distant train chugging down the tracks.

Art has the power to render sorrow beautiful, make loneliness a shared experience, and transform despair into hope. Only art can take the holler of a returning soldier and turn it into a shared expression and a deep, collective experience. Music, like all art, gives pain and our most wrenching emotions voice, language, and form, so it can be recognized and shared. The magic of the high lonesome sound is the magic of all art: the ability to both capture our pain and deliver us from it at the same time.

When we hear someone else sing about the jagged edges of heartache or the unspeakable nature of grief, we immediately know we're not the only ones in pain. The transformative power of art is in this sharing. Without connection or collective engagement, what we hear is simply a caged song of sorrow and despair; we find no liberation in it. It's the sharing of art that whispers, "You're not alone."

The world feels high lonesome and heartbroken to me right now. We've sorted ourselves into factions based on our politics and ideology. We've turned away from one another and toward blame and rage. We're lonely and untethered. And scared. So damn scared.

But rather than coming together and sharing our experiences through song and story, we're screaming at one another from further and further away. Rather than dancing and praying together, we're running from one another. Rather than pitching wild and innovative new ideas that could potentially change everything, we're staying quiet and small in our bunkers and loud in our echo chambers.

When I look through the two-hundred-thousand-plus pieces of data my team and I have collected over the past fifteen years, I can only conclude our world is in a collective spiritual crisis. This is especially true if you think about the core of that definition of "spirituality" from *The Gifts of Imperfection*:

> Spirituality is **recognizing and celebrating** that we are all **inextricably connected** to each other by a power greater than all of us, and that our connection to that power and to one another is grounded in love and compassion.

Right now we are neither recognizing nor celebrating our inextricable connection. We are divided from others in almost every area of our lives. We're not showing up with one another in a way that acknowledges our connection. Cynicism and distrust have a stranglehold on our hearts. And rather than continuing to move toward a vision of shared power *among* people, we're witnessing a backslide to a vision of power that is the key to the autocrat's power *over* people.

Addressing this crisis will require a tremendous amount of courage. For the moment, most of us are either making the choice to protect ourselves from conflict, discomfort, and vulnerability by staying quiet, or picking sides and in the process slowly and paradoxically adopting the behavior of the people we're fighting. Either way, the choices we're making to protect our beliefs and ourselves are leaving us disconnected, afraid, and lonely. Very few people are working on connection outside the lines drawn by "their side." Finding love and true belonging in our shared humanity is going to take tremendous resolution. My hope is that this research will shed light on why our quest for true belonging requires that we brave some serious wilderness. Let's look at several of the reasons behind the crisis, starting with the birth of factions.

SORTING OURSELVES OUT

As people seek out the social settings they prefer—as they choose the group that makes them feel the most comfortable—the nation grows more politically segregated—and the benefit that ought to come with having a variety of opinions is lost to the righteousness that is the special entitlement of homogeneous groups. We all live with the results: balkanized communities whose inhabitants find other Americans to be culturally incomprehensible; a growing intolerance for political differences that has made national consensus impossible; and politics so polarized that Congress is stymied and elections are no longer just contests over policies, but bitter choices between ways of life.

—BILL BISHOP

This is a quote from Bishop's book *The Big Sort*. He wrote it in 2009, but given the state of our country after the 2016 election and what's happening across the globe, he'll likely need to call its sequel *The Biggest Sort EVER*.

Bishop's book tells the story of how we've geographically, politically, and even spiritually sorted ourselves into like-minded groups in which we silence dissent, grow more extreme in our thinking, and consume only facts that support our beliefs—making it even easier to ignore evidence that our positions are wrong. He writes, "As a result, we now live in a giant feedback loop, hearing our own thoughts about what's right and wrong bounced back to us by the television shows we watch, the newspapers and books we read, the blogs we visit online, the sermons we hear, and the neighborhoods we live in."

This sorting leads us to make assumptions about the people around us, which in turn fuels disconnection. Most recently, a friend (who clearly doesn't know me very well) told me that I should read Joe Bageant's book *Deer Hunting with Jesus.* When I asked him why, he answered, with contempt in his voice, "So you can better understand the part of America that college professors have never seen and will never understand." I thought, *You don't know a damn thing about me, my family, or where I come from.*

As fast as we're sorting ourselves, the people around us are hustling to sort us too, so they know what to do and say, and so they can decide why they should trust us or why they shouldn't. My friend was hoping a book would help me understand his America. But as it turns out, it's an America I already know well. It's full of people I love. And yet, for those sharing the preconceptions of my friend, it's an America I'm not supposed to know, much less hail from.

This kind of misperception is likely to be the case for the majority of people reading this—things are not that simple. Because we're not that simple. I'm a professor whose grandfather was a Teamster, a forklift operator at a brewery. Steve is a pediatrician whose grandmother, a Mexican immigrant, sewed dresses at a factory in downtown San Antonio.

The sorting we do to ourselves and to one another is, at best, unintentional and reflexive. At worst, it is stereotyping that dehumanizes. The paradox is that we all love the ready-made filing system, so handy when we want to quickly characterize people, but we resent it when we're the ones getting filed away.

In the months following the 2016 election and the January inauguration, thousands of emails came in from our community members asking for advice on how to handle the divisiveness that was sweeping not just through the country but also through people's living rooms. Unlike the sorted demographic of our country, my community remains pretty diverse, so the emails I received were from both sides of the aisle. They were from people explaining how they haven't spoken to their father or mother for weeks or describing how an argument over social policy led directly to a discussion about divorce.

I remember when the rhetoric was at an all-time high. This was around Thanksgiving, and the big joke was about buying plastic knives and forks for family dinners to avoid casualties during the holiday feast. All I could think about then was Veronica Roth's dystopian novel *Divergent*, in which people choose factions based on their personalities. The axiom was: "Faction before blood. More than family, our factions are where we belong." Now that's scary. But what's even scarier is that it's starting to edge closer to our reality than the nightmarish fiction it was conceived to be.

Walking away from people we know and love because of our support for strangers we really don't know, can barely believe, and definitely don't love, who for sure won't be there to drive us to chemo or bring over food when the kids are sick—that's the shadow side of sorting. Family is the one group that most of us choose to negotiate rather than "sort out of our lives." Even if the polarizing politics of recent events has unmasked some core value differences between us and the people we love, severing that connection feels like the last resort—a consequence implemented only after vulnerable, tough conversations and boundary settings have failed entirely.

For twenty years, I've had the great privilege of teaching at the University of Houston. It is the most racially and ethnically diverse research university in the United States. A couple of semesters ago, I asked a class of sixty graduate students—a group reflecting the amazing diversity of our university in terms of race, sexual orientation and identity, and cultural background—if their beliefs were aligned with their grandmother's or grandfather's political, social, and cultural beliefs. About 15 percent of the students said yes or pretty close. Some 85 percent of students described everything from mild embarrassment to mortification when it came to the politics of their family members.

One African American student explained how he saw eye to eye with his grandparents on just about every issue except the one that was most important for him—he couldn't come out to his grandfather despite the fact that his entire family knew he was gay. His grandfather was a retired pastor and was "dug in" around homosexuality. A white student talked about her father's habit of addressing waiters in Mexican restaurants with "Hola, Pancho!" She had a Latino boyfriend and said it was humiliating. But when I asked if they hated their grandparents or were willing to sever relationships with family members over the political and social divides, the answer was *no* across the board. It is, of course, more complicated than that.

So here's the big question: Wouldn't you think that all of the sorting by politics and beliefs we've been doing would lead to more social interaction? If we've hunkered down ideologically and geographically with people who we perceive to be just like us, doesn't that mean that we've surrounded ourselves with friends and people with whom we feel deeply connected? Shouldn't "You're either with us or against us" have led to closer ties among the like-minded? The answer to these questions is a resounding and surprising *no*. **At the same time sorting is on the rise, so is loneliness.**

According to Bishop, in 1976 less than 25 percent of Americans lived in places where the presidential election was a landslide. In other words, we lived next door to, and attended school and worshiped with, people who held different beliefs than ours. We were ideologically diverse. In contrast, in 2016, 80 percent of U.S. counties gave either Donald Trump or Hillary Clinton a landslide victory. Most of us no longer even live near people who are all that different from us in terms of political and social beliefs.

Now let's compare these numbers to what's happening in the realm of loneliness. In 1980 approximately 20 percent of Americans reported feeling lonely. Today, it's more than double that percentage. And this is not just a local issue. Rates of loneliness are rapidly increasing in countries around the world.

Clearly, selecting like-minded friends and neighbors and separating ourselves as much as possible from people whom we think of as different from us has not delivered that deep sense of belonging that we are hardwired to crave. To understand this, we have to better understand what it means to be lonely and how the loneliness epidemic is affecting the way we show up with one another.

ON THE OUTSIDE LOOKING IN

The neuroscience researcher John Cacioppo of the University of Chicago has been studying loneliness for over twenty years. He defines loneliness as "perceived social isolation." We experience loneliness when we feel disconnected. Maybe we've been pushed to the outside of a group that we value, or maybe we're lacking a sense of true belonging. At the heart of loneliness is the absence of meaningful social interaction—an intimate relationship, friendships, family gatherings, or even community or work group connections.

It's important to note that *loneliness* and *being alone* are very different things. Being alone or inhabiting solitude can be a powerful and healing thing. As an introvert, I deeply value alone time, and I often feel the loneliest when I'm with other people. In our house, we call that sense of being disconnected "the lonely feeling."

I can't tell you the number of times I've called Steve from the road and said, "I've got the lonely feeling." The cure is normally a quick chat with him and the kids. It seems counterintuitive, but Steve then usually advises, "You may need some time alone in your hotel room." To me it's a great cure. I don't think there's anything lonelier than being with people and feeling alone.

Our family uses the term "the lonely feeling" to describe all types of things. It's not unusual for Ellen or Charlie to say, "I don't like that restaurant. It gives me the lonely feeling," or, "Can my friend spend the night here? Her house gives me the lonely feeling."

When the four of us tried to drill down on what "the lonely feeling" meant for our family, we all agreed that we get the lonely feeling in places that don't feel alive with connection. For that reason, I think places themselves, not just people, can hold those feelings of disconnection too. Sometimes a place can feel lonely because of some sense of a lack of closeness in the relationships that happen in that space. Other times, I think the inability to visualize yourself in connection with people you care about in a particular place makes a space feel lonely on its own.

While there's deep alignment between what I've found in my research and what Cacioppo has found, it wasn't until I processed his work that I fully understood the important role loneliness plays in our lives. He explains that as members of a social species, we don't derive strength from our rugged individualism, but rather from our collective ability to plan, communicate, and work together. Our neural, hormonal, and genetic makeup support interdependence over independence. He explains, "To grow to adulthood as a social species, including humans, is not to become autonomous and solitary, it's to become the one on whom others can depend. Whether we know it or not, our brain and biology have been shaped to favor this outcome." Of course we're a social species. That's why connection matters. It's why shame is so painful and debilitating. It's why we're wired for belonging.

Cacioppo explains how the biological machinery of our

brains warns us when our ability to thrive and prosper is threatened. Hunger is a warning that our blood sugar is low and we need to eat. Thirst warns us that we need to drink to avoid dehydration. Pain alerts us to potential tissue damage. And loneliness tells us that we need social connection—something as critical to our well-being as food and water. He explains, "Denying you feel lonely makes no more sense than denying you feel hunger."

Yet we do deny our loneliness. As someone who studies shame, I find myself back in territory that I know well. We feel shame around being lonely—as if feeling lonely means there's something wrong with us. We feel shame even when our loneliness is caused by grief, loss, or heartbreak. Cacioppo believes much of the stigma around loneliness comes from how we have defined it and talked about it for years. We used to define loneliness as a "gnawing, chronic disease without redeeming features." It was equated with shyness, depression, being a loner or antisocial, or possessing bad social skills. He gives a great example of this by noting how we often use the term "loner" to describe a criminal or bad guy.

Cacioppo explains that loneliness is not just a "sad" condition—it's a dangerous one. The brains of social species have evolved to respond to the feeling of being pushed to the social perimeter—being on the outside—by going into self-preservation mode. When we feel isolated, disconnected, and lonely, we try to protect ourselves. In that mode, we want to connect, but our brain is attempting to override connection with self-protection. That means less empathy, more defensiveness, more numbing, and less sleeping. In *Rising Strong*, I wrote about how the brain's self-protection mode often ramps up the stories we tell ourselves about what's happening, creating stories that are often not true or exaggerate our worst fears and insecurities. Unchecked loneliness fuels continued loneliness by keeping us afraid to reach out.

To combat loneliness, we must first learn how to identify it and to have the courage to see that experience as a warning sign. Our response to that warning sign should be to find connection. That doesn't necessarily mean joining a bunch of groups or checking in with dozens of friends. Numerous studies confirm that it's not the quantity of friends but the quality of a few relationships that actually matters.

If you're anything like me, and you find yourself questioning the idea that starvation and loneliness are equally life-threatening, let me share the study that really brought all of this together for me. In a meta-analysis of studies on loneliness, researchers Julianne Holt-Lunstad, Timothy B. Smith, and J. Bradley Layton found the following: Living with air pollution increases your odds of dying early by 5 percent. Living with obesity, 20 percent. Excessive drinking, 30 percent. And living with loneliness? It increases our odds of dying early by 45 percent.

FEAR IS HOW WE GOT HERE

So how did we get so sorted and lonely? We can't assume that sorting ourselves is the reason we've become lonelier. That's not how research works. We can't just make that leap. We can, however, acknowledge that we're in trouble in a number of dimensions that may be related, and we need to understand all of them if we want to change that.

Any answer to the question "How did we get here?" is certain to be complex. But if I had to identify one core variable that drives and magnifies our compulsion to sort ourselves into factions while at the same time cutting ourselves off from real connection with other people, my answer would be fear. Fear of vulnerability. Fear of getting hurt. Fear of the pain of disconnection. Fear of criticism and failure. Fear of conflict. Fear of not measuring up. *Fear.*

I started my research six months before 9/11, and as I've written elsewhere, I've watched fear change us. I have watched fear ride roughshod over our families, organizations, and communities. Our national conversation is centered on "What should we fear?" and "Who should we blame?"

I'm not an expert on terrorism, but I've studied fear for over fifteen years, and here's what I can tell you: Terrorism is time-released fear. The ultimate goal of both global and domestic terrorism is to conduct strikes that embed fear so deeply in the heart of a community that fear becomes a way of life. This unconscious way of living then fuels so much anger and blame that people start to turn on one another. Terrorism is most effective when we allow fear to take root in our culture. Then it's only a matter of time before we become fractured, isolated, and driven by our perceptions of scarcity. While the trends in sorting and loneliness predate 9/11, data show that they've grown significantly in the past fifteen years.

In a hardwired way, the initial trauma and devastation of violence unites human beings for a relatively short period of time. If during that initial period of unity we're allowed to talk openly about our collective grief and fear—if we turn to one another in a vulnerable and loving way, while at the same time seeking justice and accountability—it can be the start to a very long healing process. If, however, what unites us is a combination of shared hatred and stifled fear that's eventually expressed as blame, we're in trouble. If leaders race too quickly to serve up an ideological enemy that we can rally against rather than methodically identifying the actual perpetrator, what we experience is an emotional diversion away from the unraveling that's really happening in our homes and communities.

The flags are flying from every porch and the social media memes are trending, all while fear is burrowing and metastasizing. What feels like a rallying movement is really a cover for fear, which can then start spreading over the landscape and seeping into the fault lines of our country. As fear hardens, it expands and becomes less of a protective barrier and more of a solidifying division. It forces its way down in the gaps and tears apart our social foundation, already weakened with those delicate cracks.

And it's not just global and domestic terrorism that embeds fear in our cultures. Pervasive, random gun violence, and systemic attacks against groups of people, and the growing vitriol on social media—all of these send fear, like hot lava, flowing across our communities, filling in the holes and eventually working to ravage already fragile and broken places.

In the case of the United States, our three greatest fault lines—cracks that have grown and deepened due to willful neglect and a collective lack of courage—are race, gender, and class. The fear and uncertainty flowing from collective trauma of all kinds have exposed those gaping wounds in a way that's been both profoundly polarizing *and* necessary.

These are conversations that need to happen; this is discomfort that must be felt. *Still*, as much as it's time to confront these and other issues, we have to acknowledge that our lack of tolerance for vulnerable, tough conversations is driving our self-sorting and disconnection.

Can we find our way back to ourselves and to each other, and still keep fighting for what we believe in? No and yes. No, not everyone will be able to do both, simply because some people will continue to believe that fighting for what they need means denying the humanity of others. That makes connecting outside our bunkers impossible. I do believe, however, that most of us can build connection across difference and fight for our beliefs if we're willing to listen and lean in to vulnerability. Mercifully, it will take only a critical mass of people who believe in finding love and connection across difference to change everything. But if we're not even willing to try, the value of what we're fighting for will be profoundly diminished.

The data that emerged from the research on true belonging can start to connect some of the dots around why we're sorted but lonely, and perhaps contribute new insight into how we can reclaim authenticity and connection. True belonging has no bunkers. We have to step out from behind the barricades of self-preservation and brave the wild.

Huddled behind the bunkers, we don't have to worry about being vulnerable or brave or trusting. We just have to toe the party line. Except doing that is not working. Ideological bunkers protect us from everything *except* loneliness and disconnection. In other words, we're not protected from the worst heartbreaks of all.

In the remainder of this book, we're going to look at how we can reclaim human connection and true belonging in the midst of sorting and withdrawal. We have to find our way back to one another or fear wins. If you've read my work before, you'll know that it is not going to be easy. Like all meaningful endeavors, it is going to require vulnerability and the willingness to choose courage over comfort. We'll have to get through, or even better, learn how to *become* the wilderness.

High lonesome can be a beautiful and powerful place if we can own our pain and share it instead of inflicting pain on others. And if we can find a way to *feel* hurt rather than *spread* hurt, we can change. I believe in a world where we can make and share art and words that will help us find our way back to one another. Then instead of yelling from afar and refusing to help each other when we're struggling, we'll find the courage to show up for each other. As Townes Van Zandt sings in one of my favorite high lonesome songs, "If I Needed You":

> *I would come to you,*
> *I would swim the seas*
> *for to ease your pain.*

FOUR

People Are Hard to Hate
Close Up. Move In.

I imagine one of the reasons people cling to their hates so
stubbornly is because they sense, once hate is gone, they will be
forced to deal with pain.
—JAMES A. BALDWIN

If we zoom way out and take a wide-angle shot of our world that's increasingly defined by twenty-four-hour news, politics, and social media, we see a whole lot of hatred. We see posturing, name-calling, and people trading humiliations. We see politicians making laws that their own resources will exempt them from having to follow, and behaving in ways that would cost most of us our jobs, our families, and our dignity. On social media we see opinions disembodied from accountability, truth, and, worst of all, identity.

But when we zoom in on our own life, the picture changes from a distant, raging, and atrophying heart to the beating pulse of our everyday existence. We feel love and we know pain. We feel hope and we know struggle. We see beauty and we survive trauma. We don't all have the protection of privilege and the luxury of anonymity. We're trying to build connected and loving lives while we pack lunches, drive carpools, go to jobs, and push into as many moments of joy as we can.

As the larger world engages in what feels like a complete collapse of moral judgment and productive communication, the women and men I interviewed who had the strongest sense of true belonging stayed *zoomed in*. They didn't ignore what was happening in the world, nor did they stop advocating for their beliefs. They did, however, commit to assessing their lives and forming their opinions of people based on their actual, in-person experiences. They worked against the trap that most of us have fallen into: *I can hate large groups of strangers, because the members of those groups who I happen to know and like are the rare exceptions.*

Let's take a look at three examples from research participants.

The political rhetoric: *Democrats are such losers.*

Your experience: As a lifelong conservative, this sounds about right. But what about your closest friend at work—the one who drove you to the hospital when you got the call that your husband had a heart attack at the gym and was being rushed to the ER? The one who sat with you in the CICU then raced to pick up your kids from school and take them to her house? The one who helped you plan the funeral and shouldered your workload while you were out? *She's* not a loser. In fact, you love her. And she's a Democrat.

The political rhetoric: *Republicans are selfish assholes.*

Your experience: You totally agree! *Except* for your son-in-law, who is a loving and wonderful husband to your son and the most amazing father to your granddaughter. Thank God he's in the family. Even more than your son, he's the one who sends you and your wife all of the cute pictures and keeps you connected to your sweet granddaughter. *He's* not selfish. *He's* not an asshole. And he's a Republican.

The political rhetoric: *Anti-abortion activists are hypo-crites and closed-minded fundamentalists.*

Your experience: As a feminist activist, you couldn't agree more! Except for that great teacher you had in your Catholic high school. She had more integrity than anyone you know, and she constantly encouraged you to think crit-ically about tough issues, even when it meant disagreeing with her. She's actually the one who taught you how to be an effective activist. *She's* not a hypocrite or closed-minded. And she's pro-life.

What if what we experience close up is real, and what we hear on the news and from the mouths of politicians who are jockeying for power needs to be questioned? It is not easy to hate people close up. And when we are in pain and fear, anger and hate are our go-to emotions. Almost everyone I've ever interviewed or known will tell you that it's easier to be pissed off than it is to be hurt or scared.

I sometimes imagine what it would be like if I could put the entire world into a Word document and do a "find and replace" with the words and actions of hate versus pain. If I could replace the Sandy Hook deniers' hate with pain, and my own hate for them with my own pain about the kind of world we live in where people do things like this. What would that conversation be like? Would it work? Would it work to ask the white supremacists about the pain that drives their hate, and in turn creates so much pain and fear for others?

Sometimes I'll admit: I don't give a damn. There were periods during this research process when I felt like screaming: *You keep your true belonging! I'll keep my hate!* My daughter got a book on "going to college" and the first three chapters were essentially lessons in how not to get sexually assaulted. Do I really care about the pain that drives the drunk, violent assholes who make college campuses so dangerous that female students need a book about how to avoid those people? No. *Screw you and screw the pain of the people who are causing pain. I will hold on to my sweet, self-righteous rage.*

But to what end? Not caring about our own pain and the pain of others is not working. How much longer are we willing to keep pulling drowning people out of the river one by one, rather than walking to the headwaters of the river to find the source of the pain? What will it take for us to let go of that earned self-righteousness and travel together to the cradle of the pain that is throwing all of us in at such a rate that we couldn't possibly save everyone?

Pain is unrelenting. It will get our attention. Despite our attempts to drown it in addiction, to physically beat it out of one another, to suffocate it with success and material trappings, or to strangle it with our hate, pain will find a way to make itself known.

Pain will subside only when we acknowledge it and care

for it. Addressing it with love and compassion would take only a minuscule percentage of the energy it takes to fight it, but approaching pain head-on is terrifying. Most of us were not taught how to recognize pain, name it, and be with it. Our families and culture believed that the vulnerability that it takes to acknowledge pain was weakness, so we were taught anger, rage, and denial instead. But what we know now is that when we deny our emotion, it owns us. When we own our emotion, we can rebuild and find our way through the pain.

Sometimes owning our pain and bearing witness to struggle means getting angry. When we deny ourselves the right to be angry, we deny our pain. There are a lot of coded shame messages in the rhetoric of "Why so hostile?" "Don't get hysterical," "I'm sensing so much anger!" and "Don't take it so personally." All of these responses are normally code for *Your emotion or opinion is making me uncomfortable* or *Suck it up and stay quiet.*

One response to this is "Get angry and stay angry!" I haven't seen that advice borne out in the research. What I've found is that, yes, we all have the right and need to feel and own our anger. It's an important human experience. *And* it's critical to recognize that maintaining any level of rage, anger, or contempt (that favorite concoction of a little anger and a little disgust) over a long period of time is not sustainable.

Anger is a catalyst. Holding on to it will make us exhausted and sick. Internalizing anger will take away our joy and spirit; externalizing anger will make us less effective in our attempts to create change and forge connection. It's an emotion that we need to transform into something life-giving: courage, love, change, compassion, justice. Or sometimes anger can mask a far more difficult emotion like grief, regret, or shame, and we need to use it to dig into what we're really feeling. Either way, anger is a powerful catalyst but a life-sucking companion.

I can't think of a more powerful example than the sentence, "You will not have my hate." In November 2015, Antoine Leiris's wife, Hélène, was killed by terrorists at the Bataclan theater in Paris along with eighty-eight other people. Two days after the attacks, in an open letter to his wife's killers posted on Facebook, Leiris wrote:

> On Friday night, you stole the life of an exceptional being, the love of my life, the mother of my son, but you will not have my hate. I don't know who you are and I don't want to know. You are dead souls. If that God for whom you blindly kill made us in his image, every bullet in my wife's body will have been a wound in his heart.
>
> So, no, I will not give you the satisfaction of hating you. That is what you want, but to respond to your hate with anger would be to yield to the same ignorance that made you what you are. You want me to be scared, to see my fellow citizens through suspicious eyes, to sacrifice my freedom for security. You have failed. I will not change.

Leiris continues:

There are only two of us—my son and myself—but we are stronger than all the armies of the world. Anyway, I don't have any more time to waste on you, as I must go to see Melvil, who is waking up from his nap. He is only seventeen months old. He will eat his snack as he does every day, then we will play as we do every day, and all his life this little boy will defy you by being happy and free. Because you will not have his hate either.

Courage is forged in pain, but not in all pain. Pain that is denied or ignored becomes fear or hate. Anger that is never transformed becomes resentment and bitterness. I love what Nobel Peace Prize laureate Kailash Satyarthi says in his 2015 TED talk:

Anger is within each one of you, and I will share a secret for a few seconds: that if we are confined in the narrow shells of egos, and the circles of selfishness, then the anger will turn out to be hatred, violence, revenge, destruction. But if we are able to break the circles, then the same anger could turn into a great power. We can break the circles by using our inherent compassion and connect with the world through compassion to make this world better. That same anger could be transformed into it.

We pay for hate with our lives, and that's too big a price to pay.

THERE ARE ALWAYS BOUNDARIES. EVEN IN THE WILDERNESS.

When we commit to getting closer, we're committing to eventually experiencing real, face-to-face conflict. Whether it's over dinner, at work, or in the grocery line, in-person conflict is always hard and uncomfortable. And when it comes to family—it's even harder and more painful. If your family is anything like mine, you've been required to summon love and decency in the face of emotions that range from minor frustration to rage.

Maintaining the courage to stand alone when necessary in the midst of family or community or angry strangers feels like an untamed wilderness. When I get to the point where I'm like, *Screw this! It's just too hard. I'm too lost!* I hear Maya Angelou's words again: *The price is high. The reward is great.*

But here's a question that came up for me during this research: Where is the line? *Is* there a line in the wilderness between what behavior is tolerable and what isn't? The reward may be great, but do I have to put up with someone tearing me down or questioning my actual right to exist? Is there a line that shouldn't be crossed? The answer is yes.

Participants who put true belonging into practice talked openly about their boundaries. In fact, this research confirmed what I found in my earlier work: The clearer and more respected the boundaries, the higher the level of empathy and compassion for others. Fewer clear boundaries, less openness. It's hard to stay kind-hearted when you feel people are taking advantage of you or threatening you.

As I looked through the data, I saw that the line was drawn at physical safety and at what people were calling *emotional safety*. Physical safety made sense. Physical safety is one of the nonnegotiable prerequisites for vulnerability. We can't allow ourselves to be vulnerable and open if we're not physically safe.

Emotional safety was a little more ambiguous. This is especially so in a world where the term "emotional safety" is often used to mean *I don't have to listen to any point of view that's different from mine, that I don't like, that I think is wrong, that will hurt my feelings, or that is not up to my standards of political correctness.* I needed to probe deeper for clarity.

When I asked participants for examples of feeling emotionally unsafe or threatened, a clear pattern emerged. They weren't talking about getting their feelings hurt or being forced to listen to dissenting opinion; they were talking about *dehumanizing* language and behavior. I recognized this immediately. I've studied dehumanization and seen it in my work for over a decade.

David Smith, the author of *Less Than Human*, explains that dehumanization is a response to conflicting motives. We want to harm a group of people, but it goes against our wiring as members of a social species to actually harm, kill, torture, or degrade other humans. Smith explains that there are very deep and natural inhibitions that prevent us from treating other people like animals, game, or dangerous predators. He writes, "Dehumanization is a way of subverting those inhibitions."

Dehumanization is a process. I think Michelle Maiese, the chair of the philosophy department at Emmanuel College, lays it out in a way that makes sense, so I'll use some of her work here to walk us through it. Maiese defines dehumanization as "the psychological process of demonizing the enemy, making them seem less than human and hence not worthy of humane treatment." Dehumanizing often starts with creating an *enemy image*. As we take sides, lose trust, and get angrier and angrier, we not only solidify an idea of our enemy, but also start to lose our ability to listen, communicate, and practice even a modicum of empathy.

Once we see people on "the other side" of a conflict as morally inferior and even dangerous, the conflict starts being framed as good versus evil. Maiese writes, "Once the parties have framed the conflict in this way, their positions become more rigid. In some cases, zero-sum thinking develops as parties come to believe that they must either secure their own victory or face defeat. New goals to punish or destroy the opponent arise, and in some cases more militant leadership comes into power."

Dehumanization has fueled innumerable acts of violence, human rights violations, war crimes, and genocides. It makes slavery, torture, and human trafficking possible. Dehumanizing others is the process by which we become accepting of violations against human nature, the human spirit, and, for many of us, violations against the central tenets of our faith.

How does this happen? Maiese explains that most of us believe that people's basic human rights should not be violated—that crimes like murder, rape, and torture are wrong. Successful dehumanizing, however, creates *moral exclusion*. Groups targeted based on their identity—gender, ideology, skin color, ethnicity, religion, age—are depicted as "less than" or criminal or even evil. The targeted group eventually falls out of the scope of who is naturally protected by our moral code. This is moral exclusion, and dehumanization is at its core.

Dehumanizing always starts with language, often followed by images. We see this throughout history. During the Holocaust, Nazis described Jews as *Untermenschen*—subhuman. They called Jews rats and depicted them as disease-carrying rodents in everything from military pamphlets to children's books. Hutus involved in the Rwanda genocide called Tutsis cockroaches. Indigenous people are often referred to as savages. Serbs called Bosnians aliens. Slave owners throughout history considered slaves subhuman animals.

I know it's hard to believe that we ourselves could ever get to a place where we would exclude people from equal moral treatment, from our basic moral values, but we're fighting biology here. We're hardwired to believe what we see and to attach meaning to the words we hear. We can't pretend that every citizen who participated in or was a bystander to human atrocities was a violent psychopath. That's not possible, it's not true, and it misses the point. The point is that we are all vulnerable to the slow and insidious practice of dehumanizing, therefore we are all responsible for recognizing it and stopping it.

THE COURAGE TO EMBRACE OUR HUMANITY

Because so many time-worn systems of power have placed certain people outside the realm of what we see as human, much of our work now is more a matter of "rehumanizing." That starts in the same place dehumanizing starts—with words and images. Today we are edging closer and closer to a world where political and ideological discourse has become an exercise in dehumanization. And social media are the primary platforms for our dehumanizing behavior. On Twitter and Facebook we can rapidly push the people with whom we disagree into the dangerous territory of moral exclusion, with little to no accountability, and often in complete anonymity.

Here's what I believe:

1. If you are offended or hurt when you hear Hillary Clinton or Maxine Waters called bitch, whore, or the c-word, you should be equally offended and hurt when you hear those same words used to describe Ivanka Trump, Kellyanne Conway, or Theresa May.
2. If you felt belittled when Hillary Clinton called Trump supporters "a basket of deplorables" then you

should have felt equally concerned when Eric Trump said "Democrats aren't even human."

3. When the president of the United States calls women dogs or talks about grabbing pussy, we should get chills down our spine and resistance flowing through our veins. When people call the president of the United States a pig, we should reject that language regardless of our politics and demand discourse that doesn't make people subhuman.

4. When we hear people referred to as animals or aliens, we should immediately wonder, "Is this an attempt to reduce someone's humanity so we can get away with hurting them or denying them basic human rights?"

5. If you're offended by a meme of Trump Photoshopped to look like Hitler, then you shouldn't have Obama Photoshopped to look like the Joker on your Facebook feed.

There is a line. It's etched from dignity. And raging, fearful people from the right and left are crossing it at unprecedented rates every single day. We must never tolerate dehumanization—the primary instrument of violence that has been used in every genocide recorded throughout history.

When we engage in dehumanizing rhetoric or promote dehumanizing images, we diminish our own humanity in the process. When we reduce Muslim people to terrorists or Mexicans to "illegals" or police officers to pigs, it says nothing at all about the people we're attacking. It does, however, say volumes about who we are and the degree to which we're operating in our integrity.

Dehumanizing and holding people accountable are mutually exclusive. Humiliation and dehumanizing are not accountability or social justice tools, they're emotional off-loading at best, emotional self-indulgence at worst. And if our faith asks us to find the face of God in everyone we meet, that should include the politicians, media, and strangers on Twitter with whom we most violently disagree. When we desecrate their divinity, we desecrate our own, and we betray our faith.

Challenging ourselves to live by higher standards requires constant diligence and awareness. We're so saturated by these words and images, we're close to normalizing moral exceptions. In addition to diligence and awareness, we need courage. Dehumanizing works because people who speak out against what are often sophisticated enemy image campaigns—or people who fight to make sure that all of us are morally included and extended basic human rights—often face harsh consequences.

An important example is the debate around Black Lives Matter, Blue Lives Matter, and All Lives Matter. Can you believe that black lives matter and also care deeply about the well-being of police officers? Of course. Can you care about the well-being of police officers and at the same time be concerned about abuses of power and systemic racism in law enforcement and the criminal justice system? Yes. I have relatives who are police officers—I can't tell you how deeply I care about their safety and well-being. I do almost all of my pro bono work with the military and public servants like the police—I care. And when we care, we should all want just systems that reflect the honor and dignity of the people who serve in those systems.

But then, if it's the case that we can care about citizens and the police, shouldn't the rallying cry just be All Lives Matter? No. Because the humanity wasn't stripped from all lives the way it was stripped from the lives of black citizens. In order for slavery to work, in order for us to buy, sell, beat, and trade people like animals, Americans had to completely dehumanize slaves. And whether we directly participated in that or were simply a member of a culture that at one time normalized that behavior, it shaped us. We can't undo that level of dehumanizing in one or two generations. I believe Black Lives Matter is a movement to rehumanize black citizens in the hearts and minds of those of us who have consciously or unconsciously bought into the insidious, rampant, and ongoing devaluation of black lives. All lives matter, but not all lives need to be pulled back into moral inclusion. Not all people were subjected to the psychological process of demonizing and being made less than human so we could justify the inhumane practice of slavery.

Is there tension and vulnerability in supporting both the police and the activists? Hell, yes. It's the wilderness. But most of the criticism comes from people who are intent on forcing these false either/or dichotomies and shaming us for not hating the right people. It's definitely messier taking a nuanced stance, but it's also critically important to true belonging.

Another example of straddling the tension of supporting a system we love and holding it accountable comes from one of the research participants, a former athlete from Penn State. He took a strong stand as an advocate for the abuse survivors who suffered due to the silence of the football program and Joe Paterno's protection of Jerry Sandusky. He said he couldn't believe how hateful some of his friends were, friends he'd known for thirty years. He said, "When you love a place like we love Penn [State], you fight to make it better, to own our problems and fix them. You don't pretend that everything's okay. That's not loyalty or love, that's fear."

When the culture of any organization mandates that it is more important to protect the reputation of a system and those in power than it is to protect the basic human dignity of the individuals who serve that system or who are served by that system, you can be certain that the shame is systemic, the money is driving ethics, and the accountability is all but dead. This is true in corporations, nonprofits, universities, governments, faith communities, schools, families, and sports programs. If you think back on any major scandal fueled by cover-ups, you'll see this same pattern. And the restitution and resolution of cover-ups almost always happens in the wilderness—when one person steps outside their bunker and speaks their truth.

As we think about our journey from "fitting in" to striding into the wilderness of true belonging, we will be well served by understanding and recognizing the boundaries of respecting everyone's physical safety, and not participating in experiences or communities that utilize language and/or engage in behaviors that dehumanize people. I think calling the latter "emotional safety" is inaccurate. We're not talking about hurt feelings; we're talking about the very foundation of physical danger and violence.

CONFLICT TRANSFORMATION

In addition to the courage to be vulnerable, and the willingness to practice our BRAVING skills, moving closer means we need tools for navigating conflict. I asked my friend and colleague Dr. Michelle Buck to help us out. Buck is a clinical professor of leadership at the Kellogg School of Management at Northwestern University, where she served as the school's first director of leadership initiatives. She's spent the past twenty years teaching conflict transformation. Her approach has the potential to change how we handle ourselves in conflict. Below is my interview with her. I left it in this format because I want you to read her words directly—they're powerful.

Sometimes when I get overwhelmed, my default is "agree to disagree" and shut it down. What do you think about that approach?
People often silence themselves, or "agree to disagree" without fully exploring the actual nature of the disagreement, for the sake of protecting a relationship and maintaining connection. But when we avoid certain conversations, and never fully learn how the other person feels about all of

the issues, we sometimes end up making assumptions that not only perpetuate but deepen misunderstandings, and that can generate resentment. These results are sometimes worse for the relationship than just having the so-called "argument" would be. The key is to learn how to navigate conflicts or differences of opinion in a way that deepens mutual understanding, even if two people still disagree. Imagine that . . . after a meaningful conversation, two people could actually have increased mutual understanding, greater mutual respect, and better connection, but still completely disagree. This is very different from *avoiding* a conversation and not learning more about the other party.

So if we decide to be brave and stay in the conversation, how do we push through the vulnerability and stay civil?
One of the key pieces of advice I give my executive and graduate students is to explicitly address the underlying *intentions*. What is the conversation about, and what is it *really* about? This sounds simple, but tends to be easier said than done. The intention is the deepest-level reason why the topic is so important to the person. We have to understand what truly matters to us, and learn why this topic is so important to the other person as well. For example, two family members may bitterly disagree about the planning of a family event. One or both of them may have an underlying intention of wanting to create more opportunities for the family to stay connected, which may sound very different than the details of the disagreement. Speaking our intention does not mean

that we will suddenly have the same preferences or opinions, but it often helps us navigate difficult conversations and maintain or build connection by actually understanding each other's motives and interests more closely.

One of my worst defenses when I get anxious or fearful in conflict is to "put people on the stand." I break into vicious lawyer mode and depose people rather than listening. "Last week you said this. Now you're saying this. Are you lying now or were you lying then?" It's terrible and always ends badly but it's how I get to "being right." What's the solution?

That's a common strategy for people. But if you want to transform a disagreement into an opportunity for connection, you need to distinguish between past, present, and future. When disagreements revolve around what happened in the past, it's easy to fall into countless volleys of "you said . . . I said" back and forth. Focusing on what did or didn't happen in the past, or what past events led to the current situation, usually increases tension and decreases connection. A critical first step is to shift the focus to "Where are we *now*?" and the most important turning point comes when we focus on the future. What are we trying to accomplish for the future? What do we want our relationship to be going forward, and what do we need to do, even if we still disagree, to create that future? What do we want for our family in the future . . . or for our team, or our faith community, or our industry? This shift in focus does not necessarily mean we agree, but it may help us identify agreement about a shared future that we want to create together.

I like that you use the term "conflict *transformation*," not *"resolution."* It feels more about connection in some way to me. What's the difference?
In all of my work, I choose to focus on "conflict transformation," rather than the more traditional term "conflict resolution." To me, the latter suggests going back to a previous state of affairs, and has a connotation that there may be a winner or a loser. How will this disagreement be resolved? Whose solution will be selected as the "better" one? In contrast, I choose to focus on "conflict transformation," suggesting that by creatively navigating the conversational landscape of differences and disagreements, we have the opportunity to create something new. At a minimum, we learn more about each other than before. Ideally, we may find new possibilities that had not even been considered before. Conflict transformation is about creating deeper understanding. It requires perspective-taking. As a result, it enables greater connection, whether or not there is agreement.

Last question! I spend most of my time preparing my argument when other people are talking. I want to be ready to "counter." Yet I hate it when people do that to me. I can tell when someone's not really listening. It feels terrible. How can you slow things down in the midst of conflict?
One of the most essential steps in this transformative com-

munication, and perhaps the most courageous, is not only to be open-minded, but to listen with desire to learn more about the other person's perspective. I believe, and tell my students, one of the most courageous things to say in an uncomfortable conversation is *"Tell me more."* Exactly when we want to turn away and change the topic, or just end the conversation, or *counter,* as you say, we also have the opportunity to ask what else we need to know to fully understand the other person's perspective. *Help me understand why this is so important to you,* or *help me understand why you don't agree with a particular idea.* And then we have to listen. Really listen. Listen to understand, not about agreeing or disagreeing. We have to listen to understand in the same way we want to be understood.

COURAGE AND POWER FROM PAIN: AN INTERVIEW WITH VIOLA DAVIS

I want to end this chapter with an interview that I did with Viola Davis. You may know Viola from her performances in *The Help, How to Get Away with Murder,* and *Fences* (for which she won an Oscar for best supporting actress). She is the first black actor to win the Triple Crown of acting—the Emmy, Tony, and Oscar. In 2017, she was listed by *Time* magazine as one of the one hundred most influential people in the world.

Viola's story exemplifies the power of courage in the face of pain, vulnerability in the face of fear, and how living and loving close up leads to true belonging.

When I asked Viola to tell me about the beginning of her journey into true belonging, she told me, "I spent the first three-quarters of my life feeling like a square peg in a round hole. I did not physically fit in. I lived in an Irish Catholic area of Rhode Island—white girls with long blond hair. I was a kinky-haired girl with dark skin who spoke different. I wasn't pretty. I carried the trauma of growing up in abject poverty—the daughter of a violent alcoholic. I was a bed-wetter until I was twelve or thirteen. I smelled. Teachers complained about the smell and sent me to the nurse's office. I was wrong. This was my beginning.

"My language for belonging was about survival: Can I take a hot shower? Is there food today? Will my dad kill my mom? Will there be rats in the house?

"I had no tools—I carried this trauma, fear, anxiety, and the inability to speak up for myself into my adult life. All of it was deeply rooted in shame. I spent all of my energy hiding and keeping the brutality of my life secret. I carried this dysfunction with me into my adult life."

Then I asked her to tell me about taking her first steps into her wilderness. She said, "I knew I was afraid of confrontation, but it wasn't until I started doing therapy that I realized why the anxiety made speaking up almost impossible. I had an experience where I should have confronted someone who was doing something horrible to me. What I realized was, in that moment, I flashbacked to my fourteen-year-old self. I was holding my baby sister and my father was stabbing my mother in the neck with a pencil. I shouted, 'Stop it! Give me that pencil!' He did it. My father stopped and handed me the pencil. I was a child who was forced to confront an adult.

I had to take the power position before I should have needed to and before I was ready. I paid for it in fear."

Viola is someone who's made the transition from fear of the wilderness, to braving the wilderness, to becoming the wilderness. I wanted to know how that happened.

"At thirty-eight, things changed. I didn't jump out of bed one morning and everything was perfect. I've always known I was a strong woman, but I wanted 'fast-food joy'— quick, easy joy. More tools and tricks. I also could still fall back into 'not enough—not pretty enough, not thin enough, not good enough.' One day my therapist asked me a pivotal question: 'What if nothing changes—your looks, your weight, your success—would you be okay?' For the first time, I thought, *You know what? Yes, I would. I really would.*

"This is when I realized that the past was not going to define me.

"I also got married to an amazing man who really saw me. He was my gift for working so hard on myself. He was kind and I was finally vulnerable and open to that."

I asked her, "When you belong to yourself there is always going to be criticism. What's your experience with that?" Viola replied, "Acting culture can be brutal. The notes can simply say, 'Not attractive enough. Too old. Too dark-skinned. Not skinny enough.' They tell you to develop a thick skin so things don't get to you. What they don't tell you is that your thick skin will keep everything from getting out, too. Love, intimacy, vulnerability.

"I don't want that. Thick skin doesn't work anymore. I

want to be transparent and translucent. For that to work, I won't own other people's shortcomings and criticisms. I won't put what you say about me on my load."

I'm not sure there's a more poignant example of someone who was able to recognize her pain, own her story, and write a new ending that includes transforming her pain into compassion for others.

"I held my dad's hand as he died," she told me. "He died of pancreatic cancer. We had healed our relationship; we loved each other very much. When my sister and I sat with him we learned that he hated his work his entire life. For decades he groomed horses at a racetrack. We never knew he hated it. He had a second grade education. He also worked as a janitor. We never knew that's how he felt. It was devastating for us to think about the pain he endured his entire life.

"There's an unspoken message that the only stories worth telling are the stories that end up in history books. This is not true. Every story matters. My father's story *matters*. We are all worthy of telling our stories and having them heard. We all need to be seen and honored in the same way that we all need to breathe."

Viola Davis is the wilderness. I asked her if true belonging took the shape of a practice for her. She said, "Yes. Today, I live by a few simple rules:

1. I'm doing the best I can.
2. I will allow myself to be seen.
3. I apply the advice an acting coach gave me to all as-

pects of my life: Go further. Don't be afraid. Put it all out there. Don't leave anything on the floor.

4. I will not be a mystery to my daughter. She will know me and I will share my stories with her—the stories of failure, shame, and accomplishment. She will know she's not alone in that wilderness.

"This is who I am.

"This is where I am from.

"This is my mess.

"This is what it means to belong to myself."

FIVE

Speak Truth to Bullshit.
Be Civil.

Someone who lies and someone who tells the truth are playing on opposite sides, so to speak, in the same game. Each responds to the facts as he understands them, although the response of the one is guided by the authority of the truth, while the response of the other defies that authority and refuses to meet its demands. The bullshitter ignores these demands altogether. He does not reject the authority of the truth, as the liar does, and oppose himself to it. He pays no attention to it at all. By virtue of this, bullshit is a greater enemy of the truth than lies are.
—HARRY G. FRANKFURT

I'm grateful that Carl Jung reminds us that the paradox is one of our most valuable spiritual possessions, because without that reminder I'd probably just feel pissed off about this specific true belonging practice. I love the idea of speaking truth to bullshit and I believe in civility—I just think it's really hard to combine the two. In this chapter we're going to dig into what drives BS, what form it often takes, and how we stay civil when we're knee-deep in it.

BULLSHIT

Harry Frankfurt is professor emeritus of philosophy at Princeton University. He spent his career teaching at Yale, Rockefeller, and Ohio State. In 2005, he published *On Bullshit*. It's a very small book about the nature of BS, how it's different from lying, and why we're all compelled to bullshit on occasion.

I was captivated by three points that Frankfurt makes in his book and how those points accurately reflect what I found from the research participants when they talked about their struggles to maintain their authenticity and integrity when engaging in debates and discussions driven by emotion rather than shared understanding of facts. The first insight is the difference between lying and bullshitting that's explained in the quote that opens this chapter: It's helpful to think of lying as a defiance of the truth and bullshitting as a wholesale dismissal of the truth.

Second, it's advantageous to recognize how we often rely on bullshitting when we feel compelled to talk about things we don't understand. Frankfurt explains how the widespread conviction that many of us share about needing to comment or weigh in on every single issue around the globe leads to increased levels of BS. It is crazy to me that so many of us feel we need to have fact-based opinions on everything from what's happening in Sudan and Vietnam to the effects of climate change in the Netherlands and immigration policy in California.

I'm guilty too. I can't remember a time in the last year when someone asked me about an issue and I didn't weigh in with an opinion. Even if I didn't know enough about it to be insightful or even conversational, I would lean in to ideological debates based on what I guessed "my people" think about it. I also can't remember a time over the past year when I asked someone about an issue and had a person reply, "I actually don't know much about what's happening there, please tell me about it."

We don't even bother being curious anymore because somewhere, someone on "our side" has a position. In a fitting-in culture—at home, at work, or in our larger community—curiosity is seen as weakness and asking questions equates to antagonism rather than being valued as learning.

Last, Frankfurt argues that the contemporary spread of bullshit also has a deeper source: our being skeptical and denying that we can ever know the truth of how things truly are. He argues that when we give up on believing that there are actual truths that can be known and shared observable knowledge, we give up on the notion of objective inquiry. It's like we just collectively shrug our shoulders and say, "Whatever. It's too hard to get to the truth, so if I say it's true, that's good enough."

Frankfurt's astute observation of where that leads us feels prophetic in 2017. He argues that once we decide that it makes no sense to try to be true to the facts, we simply resort to being true to ourselves. This, to me, is the birthplace of one of the great bullshit problems of our time: the "you're either with us or against us" argument.

IF YOU'RE NOT WITH ME, THEN YOU'RE MY ENEMY

As I briefly touched on earlier, one of the biggest drivers of the sorting that's happening today is the proliferation of the belief that "you're either with us or you're against us." It's an emotional line that we hear everyone, from politicians to movie heroes and villains, invoke on a regular basis. It's one of the most effective political sorters, and 95 percent of the time it's an emotional and passionate rendering of bullshit. Well intentioned or not.

Benito Mussolini relied heavily on the line *"O con noi o contro di noi"* ("You're either with us or against us"). In the weeks following 9/11, both George W. Bush and Hillary Clinton told the world's citizens that they were either with us in the fight against terrorism or against us. Bush took it even further by saying, "Every nation, in every region, now has a decision to make. Either you are with us, or you are with the terrorists." And it's in our stories, too. In *Star Wars: Revenge of the Sith*, Darth Vader says to Obi-Wan Kenobi, "If you're not with me, then you're my enemy."

Normally, we use the "with me or against me" during times of significant emotional stress. Our intentions may not be to manipulate, but to force the point that we're in a situation where neutrality is dangerous. I actually agree with this point. One of my live-by quotes is from Elie Wiesel. "We must always take sides. Neutrality helps the oppressor, never the victim. Silence encourages the tormentor, never the tormented." The problem is that the emotional plea is often not based in facts, and preys on our fears of not belonging or being seen as wrong or part of the problem. We need to question how the sides are defined. *Are these really the only two options? Is this the accurate framing for this debate or is this bullshit?*

In philosophy, "you're either with us or against us" is considered a *false dichotomy* or a *false dilemma*. It's a move to force people to take sides. If other alternatives exist (and they almost always do), then that statement is factually wrong. It's turning an emotion-driven approach into weaponized belonging. And it always benefits the person throwing down the gauntlet and brandishing those forced, false choices.

The ability to think past either/or situations is the foundation of critical thinking, but still, it requires courage. Getting curious and asking questions happens outside our bunkers of certainty. For most of us, even if the "with us or against us" mandate sounds a little like oversimplified BS, it *still* feels easier and safer to pick a side. The argument is set up in a way that there's only one real option. If we stay quiet we're automatically demonized as "the other."

The only true option is to refuse to accept the terms of the argument by challenging the framing of the debate. But make no mistake; this is opting for the wilderness. Why? Because the argument is set up to silence dissent and draw lines in the sand that squelch debate, discussion, and questions—the very processes that we know lead to effective problem solving.

Our silence, however, comes at a very high individual and collective cost. Individually, we pay with our integrity. Collectively, we pay with divisiveness, and even worse, we bypass effective problem solving. Answers that have the force of emotion behind them but are not based in fact rarely provide strategic and effective solutions to nuanced problems. We normally don't set up false dilemmas because we're intentionally bullshitting; we often rely on this device when we're working from a place of fear, acute emotion, and lack of knowledge. Unfortunately, fear, acute emotion, and lack of knowledge also provide the perfect set-up for uncivil behavior. This is why the bullshit/incivility cycle can become endless.

CIVILITY

It's easier to stay civil when we're combating lying than it is when we're speaking truth to bullshit. When we're bullshitting, we aren't interested in the truth as a shared starting point. This makes arguing slippery and it makes us more susceptible to mirroring the BS behavior, which is: The truth doesn't matter, *what I think* matters. It's helpful to keep in mind Alberto Brandolini's Bullshit Asymmetry Principle or what's sometimes known as Brandolini's law: "The amount of energy needed to refute bullshit is an order of magnitude bigger than to produce it."

Sometimes calling out BS is unnecessary because there's an expectation of embellishment, like an overly polite compliment or, in the case of my Texan family, a tall tale of walking uphill to school . . . both ways, in the snow, pulling a donkey. But when the stakes are high and we need to speak truth to bullshit, I've seen two practices that increase effectiveness.

First, approach bullshitting with generosity when possible. Don't assume that people know better and they're just being malicious or mean-spirited. In highly charged discussions, we can feel shame about not having an informed opinion and these feelings of "not enough" can lead us to bullshitting our way through a conversation. We can also believe we're responding from real data and have no idea that there's nothing to back up what we're saying. Additionally, we can get so caught up in our own pain and fear that truth and fact play second fiddle to emotional pleas for understanding or agreement. Generosity, empathy, and curiosity (e.g., Where did you read this or hear this?) can go a long way in our efforts to question what we're hearing and introduce fact.

The second practice is civility. I found a definition of civility from the Institute for Civility in Government that very closely reflects how the research participants talked about civility. The organization's cofounders, Cassandra Dahnke and Tomas Spath, write:

> Civility is claiming and caring for one's identity, needs, and beliefs without degrading someone else's in the process. . . . [Civility] is about disagreeing without disrespect, seeking common ground as a starting point

for dialogue about differences, listening past one's preconceptions, and teaching others to do the same. Civility is the hard work of staying present even with those with whom we have deep-rooted and fierce disagreements. It is political in the sense that it is a necessary prerequisite for civic action. But it is political, too, in the sense that it is about negotiating interpersonal power such that everyone's voice is heard, and nobody's is ignored.

Holding what we're exploring about bullshit, false dichotomies, and civility in our heads, let's take a look at two real stories. The first is a story about an experience when I was thrown into a "with us or against us" situation around a very controversial issue and had to fight to stay civil in the midst of BS. The second is a story of how I fell prey to my own BS and unknowingly dropped my team into the "you're either with me or against me" construct. What I learned from both of these experiences changed me.

Battery-Operated Socks

I knew exactly what I wanted for my fourteenth birthday. No more Bobbie Brooks sweaters, pet rocks, Leif Garrett posters, or toe socks. I was ready for some serious teenage gifts. My list included my own set of Clairol hot rollers (the ones with the plastic cover that snapped into a travel handle), *Some Girls* by the Rolling Stones (I had lent mine to a friend and her older brother sold it for beer), a pair of Gloria Vanderbilt jeans, and a pair of Candie's shoes (those rockin' slide-on high heels that all the cool girls were wearing).

I got the hot rollers, a pair of Lee jeans, and the replacement Rolling Stones album. My parents suggested that I get a job if I wanted a pair of Gloria Vanderbilt or Jordache jeans, and that I find myself some new parents if I wanted to wear Candie's before I turned twenty. Before I retreated to my room to blast "Beast of Burden," my parents surprised me with another gift. I could tell by the box it wasn't the Candie's, but my dad's excitement was contagious so I eagerly ripped into my gift.

Battery-operated socks. Big woolly gray battery-operated socks. I must have looked confused because my dad said, "C'mon, sis! For the deer blind! So your feet don't get cold anymore."

I felt bad. I knew instantly that I'd never need those socks but I didn't know how to break the news to my dad. I was done hunting. In all of our trips, I had never shot a deer. I just couldn't bring myself to do it. I could hold my own in a dove or quail hunt, but I wasn't ever going to shoot a deer. So, for me, hunting trips were just long days in freezing blinds and cold nights in sleeping bags with all of my cousins.

I never went again and I never used my socks, but today I realize how much hunting was a part of my life growing up. Even after I'd stopped going, I still felt the communal excitement and anticipation in our house when the various seasons would open. Those dates were part of the rhythm of our family, like birthdays or holidays. And there were always family and friends visiting, and feasts of amazing food.

My dad was very serious about all things hunting. You could only shoot what was covered by your hunting license and you absolutely could not shoot anything you didn't plan to eat. These were nonnegotiable rules in my house, essentially etched into stone tablets. He had no patience for trophy hunting or the like.

In turn, we were like the Bubba Gumps of venison . . . venison steak, venison sausage, venison stew, venison jerky, venison burgers. There was nothing better than when the hunters came back from the hunting lease and twenty or thirty people would pack into our house or my aunt's house to process deer meat, make tamales, tell stories, and laugh. My dad is the youngest of six, and I have twenty-four first cousins. There were a lot of mouths to feed. Hunting and fishing were as practical and necessary as they were fun for most of us.

We all had guns. We got BB guns when we were in second or third grade and hunting rifles by fifth grade, when most of us started hunting. Gun safety was no joke. In fact, we weren't allowed to shoot a gun that we couldn't take apart, clean, and put back together.

When you grow up hunting you have a very different understanding about the reality of guns. It's not a video game—you know, and have felt, exactly what they are capable of doing. For my dad and the people we hunted with, the sentiment around automatic weapons and the big guns that people treat like toys today was simple: "You want to shoot those kinds of guns? Great! Enlist and serve."

Now that I'm a parent, I can look back and see that what was equally powerful was the combination of our family rules concerning hunting and guns, and that we weren't allowed to watch any violence on TV. I couldn't see a PG movie until I was fifteen years old. The idea of romanticizing violence was out of the question. We didn't have violent video games back then, but I can only imagine how my dad would have felt about them.

I loved and was proud of this part of my family story. And, like most kids, I assumed that everyone who was raised in a hunting and gun culture was raised with the same rules. But as I got a little older, I realized that wasn't true. As laws governing gun ownership became more and more political and polarized, I became more skeptical of the gun lobby. I watched the NRA go from being an organization that I associated with safety programs, merit badges, and charity skeet tournaments to something I didn't recognize. *Why were they positioning themselves as the people who represented families like ours while not putting any limits or parameters around responsible gun ownership?*

Despite my beliefs, my family started supporting the gun lobby while many of my friends and colleagues began vilifying all gun ownership. I quickly realized that I'd have no ideological home or community on this issue. I didn't have the language of "the wilderness" to describe how alone I felt about this. But it definitely was, and is, the wild.

Late last year, I was talking to a group of people at an event and I mentioned that my father and I were looking forward to teaching my son how to shoot skeet. One woman looked horrified and said, "I'm very surprised to hear that you're a gun lover. You don't strike me as the NRA type." If you're reading her comment as aggressive and pointed, then I've communicated it accurately. There was contempt and disgust on her face.

I replied, "I'm not sure what you mean by 'gun lover' or 'the NRA type.'" She sat straight up in her chair. "If you're teaching your child how to shoot a gun, then I'm assuming that you support gun ownership and the NRA."

There it was. The false dichotomy.

If I support gun ownership then I support the National Rifle Association. No way. I'm not buying it.

Of all of the lobbying organizations I've studied over the past twenty years, not one of them has done a better job using fear and false dichotomies than the NRA. Today's NRA rhetoric employs the ominous *they* and forces "us versus them" language over and over. *Allow anyone to buy any type of gun and ammunition, when and wherever they want, or they will break down your door, take away your guns, crush your freedom, kill everyone you love, and put an end to the American way. They are after us. They are coming.* That's the biggest bunch of bullshit I've heard since someone told me, "If you own a gun—any gun—you might as well be the one pulling the trigger in all of these terrible mass shootings." No and no.

I took a deep "don't lose your shit" breath, smiled, and

said, "You're one for two on your assumptions. I do support responsible gun ownership. I do *not* in any way support the NRA just because I support responsible gun ownership."

She looked mad and confused. "But with all the school shootings—I don't understand why you don't support gun control."

C'mon, sister.

"I absolutely do support commonsense gun laws. I believe in background checks and waiting periods. I don't believe that it should be legal to sell automatic weapons, large magazines, or armor-piercing bullets. I don't believe in campus carry. I . . ."

She was so angry at this point. She spit out, "You either support guns or you don't."

Because I was already working on this book, I said the thing that I've felt my entire life but was either too afraid to say or didn't have the words. I mustered up the most empathy I could and said, "I know that this is a hard and heartbreaking issue, but I don't think you're hearing me. I'm not going to participate in a debate where this issue is reduced to *You either support guns or you don't.* It's too important. If you want to have a longer conversation about it, I'm happy to do that. And I wouldn't be surprised if the same issues piss us off and scare us."

She excused herself and stormed away. She probably hates me. The small group of people who were standing with us may hate me. *You* may hate me. Who knows? It's not always the happy ending from some movie, but I'll take it if it's real.

Here's why the ending works for me. I knew exactly what I could have said in that moment to position myself as the darling of the group. I could have betrayed my actual beliefs and made myself the hero in a heartbeat. I could have avoided the confrontation entirely. You didn't have to be Sherlock Holmes to know that everyone standing in the group preferred no guns or, at the very least, no uncomfortable conversations about guns. I also could've opted to stay quiet. Or I could have lost my shit. But instead, I belonged to me. I did the best I could to debunk the either/or argument, I chose to be out in the open—away from the safety of the ideological bunker that the room had become. And I was decent. I was respectful to her and to myself.

I felt alone in the wilderness, but it was okay. I may not have been liked, and that didn't feel so great, but I was in my integrity. And the group may have felt betrayed by my answer or my willingness to get into a tough conversation, but still, and most important, I didn't betray myself. To know you can navigate the wilderness on your own—to know that you can stay true to your beliefs, trust yourself, and survive it—that is true belonging.

CHIEF OF STAFF

Most people are surprised to learn that in addition to my research, I lead four companies and work with a team of about twenty-five people. There's Brave Leaders Inc, The Daring Way, The Marble Jar Store, and our umbrella company, Brené Brown Education and Research Group. There's a team that manages my speaking events, another that runs

The Daring Way (our training program for helping professionals), a team that coordinates all of our volunteer and pro bono work, a team that runs our store, leaders who oversee our social work intern program, a consumer experience team, researchers, a team that develops and produces digital content, and a core team that handles our mission and operations work.

Our mission is "making the world a braver place by doing work we love with people we care about in a way that's aligned with our values." Every time I walk into our offices I wonder how I got so lucky as to have a team that believes deeply in our work and in one another. I spend most of my time with the Round-Up team, which consists of Charles (our CFO), Murdoch (my manager), and Suzanne (our president and COO).

A little over a year ago, I was so underwater with the pressures of writing, traveling to speak, teaching, trying to lead the day-to-day operations of these businesses, and researching, that the Round-Up team called an emergency offsite meeting in Galveston to see if we could come up with a solution to what was clearly an untenable situation. I was cratering so fast that Steve took off work to join us for the day. He wanted to make sure that something was going to change, and he knew delegating and letting go were deep struggles for me. It felt like five minutes ago that I was a person with a book and a blog, and suddenly I was the CEO and president. It was too much, too fast, and I was lost.

There were twelve of us, including the four members of

the Round-Up team, in Galveston. We had three agenda items at our meeting:

1. Make a comprehensive list of everything that I was doing so we could better understand what I could hand off to others,

2. Develop a strategy that would keep me above water, and

3. Put all of the ideas, plans, and strategies that lived in my head on paper so we could assess what was important and what was not.

About two hours into our meeting someone suggested that one solution to all of these problems might be bringing on someone to serve in a "chief of staff" role. Of course, when I hear "chief of staff" all I can think of is Leo Mc-Garry, President Bartlet's chief of staff on *The West Wing*. At first I laughed, but within minutes everyone was excited about the idea and I started to feel hopeful. Half an hour into the discussion, one of our team members volunteered to move into that position and I felt more relief and excitement than I had felt in a year. I was even a little teary-eyed. I was fully leaning in to this idea and when I do that, the people around me normally take notice.

I am a passionate and intense person. And despite my love of good humor and belly laughing until I cry, most people who know me well describe me as a pretty serious person. The first time I heard someone describe me as serious, it hurt my feelings. I'd always thought of myself as bubbly and whimsical, like Meg Ryan in *French Kiss*. When I finally reality-checked my personality dysmorphia with Steve he confirmed, "Kind and funny? Yes. Bubbly and whimsical? No. Serious? Almost always."

My team has shared the feedback with me that sometimes when I get passionate and intense about an idea it's like being in a "Brené wind tunnel." They say it's hard to stay standing, much less speak up. This chief of staff position felt like a lifesaver to me and I was now its greatest champion. *Cue the wind tunnel*. I looked at the group and said, "This is going to change everything. I say we start right away. No time like the present!"

I spotted a smidgen of concern on the faces of the Round-Up team, but I felt temporarily delivered from desperation and it was such a welcome feeling that I didn't much care about the drop of reservation I saw. I drew a deep breath and said, "We either try this starting right now, or we pretend that everything will be different after today even though we know it won't."

The room was quiet for a few seconds. I flipped to a new page in my journal and wrote "CoS" at the top and started numbering down the side of the page. This is where I'd start to list all of the responsibilities I could hand off to this new person so I could get at least some of my life back. When I looked up for a brief second, Suzanne had her hand in the air.

I smiled because it seemed funny to me that she was raising her hand and not just talking. I looked at her and said, "Yes, Suzanne?"

Her face was red but her eyes and voice were steady. "I want to remind everyone in this room, especially the Round-Up team, that we made a decision to never hire anyone or reassign positions in a group setting. We made a commitment to move slower and talk things through as a smaller team before we make decisions like this."

My sense of hope and possibility immediately vanished. Steve would later tell me that he had never seen someone so visibly deflate in his life. I just stared at Suzanne. My disappointment was quickly turning into anger. Before I could say a word, Suzanne said, "I don't think the options are making this decision right now or pretending that everything will be different after today when we know it won't. We will work on this until we fix it. But I believe in the commitment our team made to not make decisions under these circumstances."

We called a break and I went into the bathroom and cried. I was so tired. So desperate for help and support. And, after a five-minute sob, deeply grateful to Suzanne. She was right. I hated giving up on the magic bullet even though I knew it reeked of bullshit as it was happening. Desperate times call for desperate measures, and desperate measures are often fertilized with bullshit.

Suzanne was waiting for me as I came out of the bathroom. I thanked her for being so brave and she assured me that she knew the current situation was bad for me, bad for our work, bad for everyone, and needed to change. She promised that together we could find a new way of working.

Suzanne still describes that moment as one of the hardest in our time together. For her, questioning my decision was the absolute wilderness. She felt alone, vulnerable, and scared. And, truthfully, she was completely alone as she raised her hand in that meeting. From my perspective, it was the day I realized I could trust her with anything. I promoted Suzanne to president of Brené Brown Education and Research Group. Today she runs the day-to-day operations of the businesses. And she kicks total ass.

This experience is also when our team started to understand how important it is for us to build a culture that supports true belonging. If leaders really want people to show up, speak out, take chances, and innovate, we have to create cultures where people feel safe—where their belonging is not threatened by speaking out and they are supported when they make the decision to brave the wilderness, stand alone, and speak truth to bullshit.

It's easy to underestimate the importance of civility at work, but new research shows just how crippling incivility can be for teams and organizations. Christine Porath, an associate professor of management at Georgetown University, writes, "Incivility can fracture a team, destroying collaboration, splintering members' sense of psychological safety, and hampering team effectiveness. Belittling and demeaning comments, insults, and other rude behavior can deflate confidence, sink trust, and erode helpfulness—even for those who aren't the target of these behaviors." She cites her own research and other studies that show how implementing civility standards and enforcing them leads to higher-performing and better-functioning teams.

I had the opportunity to interview NFL coach Pete Carroll of the Seattle Seahawks for this research. When I asked him about the challenges of developing an organizational culture of true belonging, he offered what I believe is a profound insight into brave leadership:

> There's no question that it's easier to manage a "fitting-in" culture. You set standards and rules. You lead by "put up or shut up." But you miss real opportunities—especially helping your team members find their purpose. When you push a "fitting-in culture" you miss the opportunity to help people find their personal drive—what's coming from their hearts. Leading for true belonging is about creating a culture that celebrates uniqueness. What serves leaders best is understanding your players' best efforts. My job as a leader is to identify their unique gift or contribution. A strong leader pulls players toward a deep belief in themselves.

Words as Weapons

Sometimes civility takes the shape of respect and generosity. I recently taught an online class with Dr. Harriet Lerner on how to offer a true, heartfelt apology and how to accept one. It kicked my ass. I think we should broadcast these apologizing lessons over the airwaves of some Orwellian TV station so everyone in the country could learn these skills—we need them!

As Harriet invited me to practice listening and apologizing without disclaimers and exceptions, I learned that when armored up, I'd rather be right than connected and invested in my relationship. I want to win. I love being right.

The need to be right is magnified when we feel we're in hostile territory and under attack. A cultural example of this is political correctness. The history of this concept is as wild and unruly as the conversations about it have become. At this point, the term is so loaded that I think it makes more sense to talk about *inclusive language.*

Given what we know about dehumanizing, I believe inclusive language is critically important, absolutely worth the effort, and a function of civility. We often take sides when it comes to the big political debates around issues like sports team names and ignore the everyday instances that are equally diminishing. For example, let's say you've been diagnosed with anxiety and your child has attention deficit disorder. How would you feel if you overheard your doctor saying, "Yeah. I've got my anxiety disorder coming at 2 P.M., then I'm going to see the ADD kid before I go home." Proponents of inclusive language would say you're not your diagnosis; you're a person with anxiety. It matters to all of us. No one wants to be reduced.

But what's tough about the inclusive language movement is when people turn using the right language into a weapon to shame or belittle people. This came up over and over in the research. Even tools of civility can become weaponized if the intention is there. I'll share a couple of stories with you.

First there was a man in his late twenties who shared a story of driving from his home in Los Angeles to Newport Beach to visit his parents. He told me that during the morning drive he made a commitment to be more patient with and tolerant of his father. They had a long history of not getting along.

The afternoon the man arrived, he was standing in the kitchen making small talk when he asked his father, "How are your new neighbors?"

His father said, "We really like them. We've had them over for dinner a couple of times and we've become friends. They're cooking us dinner next week. They're Oriental and she's going to make her special dumplings, so your mom is really looking forward to it."

The young man told me that he ripped right into his father. "Oriental? Jesus, Dad! Are you kidding? Racist much?"

Before his father could even respond, he went back at him. "'Oriental' is so racist! Do you even know where they're from? There's no country called 'the orient.' How embarrassing!"

He said that rather than engaging, his father stood in the kitchen with his head down. When he finally looked up at his son, he was teary-eyed. "I'm sorry, son. I'm not sure what I've done or not done to make you so angry. I just can't do anything right. Nothing I do or say is good enough for you."

There was total silence.

Then his father said, "I'd stay and let you tell me what

an asshole I am, but I'm taking the neighbor I supposedly hate to pick up her husband from cataract surgery. She doesn't drive and he took a cab this morning."

During the interview, the man told me that he didn't know what to do or say so he just walked away before his dad left the kitchen.

This second story happened to me. I was teaching a half-day course on shame resilience (oh, the irony) and there were about two hundred people in the audience. At the halfway mark of the day, we took a short break. I was going through my notes when a woman walked up to me and said, "I can't tell you how much you hurt me this morning."

I was stunned. Time started slowing down and I was falling into tunnel vision—my normal shame response. Before I could open my mouth, she said, "Your work has changed my life. It saved my marriage and shaped my children. I came here today because you are an important teacher in my life. Then fifteen minutes after you start, I learn that you're an anti-Semite. I trusted you and you've proven to be a fraud."

Shame shit storm of gigantic proportion. Nightmare come true.

All I could eke out was, "I don't understand."

She said, "You said that you felt 'really gypped' during your story."

I still didn't get it. Again, I said, "I don't understand."

She got louder. "Gypped. *Gypped. Gypped!* Don't you know? How do you think you spell 'gypped'?"

It was a weird question but I was too far down the shame hole to say something helpful like, "I can see you're really angry, let's talk about it." I paused for a second to sound out the word in my head and find a word remotely close that I could use as a spelling reference. The only thing that came to mind was Jif peanut butter (of course). "Umm . . . J-I-P-P-E-D."

She yelled, "No! Nothing in the world is spelled J-I-P-P-E-D. It's spelled G-Y-P-P-E-D. Like 'gypsy.' It's an anti-Semitic term that degrades gypsies."

I had no idea. My mind was scrambling. Was I in one of those nightmare scenarios where the truth was spilling out and I couldn't control it? Did I really hate gypsies? Was I deep undercover as a politically correct social worker that really harbored hateful feelings about gypsies?

No. I just didn't know. I had no idea.

I guess the look on my face told her I wasn't lying because she said, "Oh, my God. You didn't know. You didn't do that on purpose, did you?"

At this point I was in tears.

"I'm so sorry. I didn't know. I apologize," I explained.

She hugged me and we talked about it for a few minutes. When everyone came back, I explained what I had learned and apologized to the group for using that language. But honestly, I never recovered that afternoon.

For the man visiting his father, it would have been just as easy to say, "You know, Dad, people are not using the term 'oriental' any longer. Language is changing fast—

I thought I'd let you know." If he wanted to be really empathic, he could say something like, "I'm learning every day too."

If my work really meant that much to the woman at the conference, she could have approached me with a more generous assumption. She could have said, "I don't know if you know this, but 'gypped' is a derogatory word based on a hurtful stereotype of gypsies." I would have been grateful instead of ashamed.

I don't know about you, but I want to know if I'm saying something that's hurtful. I want to be kind and thoughtful with my words because I'm keenly aware of how much they matter. Will it be awkward? Yes. Is it frustrating to have to teach people why their words are hurtful to you? Yes. Does talking about these issues require a venture into the wilderness? Yes. But it also requires that we stay vulnerable, and that's hard to do when we turn words into weapons.

BRAVING

Speaking truth to bullshit and practicing civility start with knowing ourselves and knowing the behaviors and issues that both push into our own BS or get in the way of being civil. If we go back to BRAVING and our trust checklist, these situations require a keen eye on:

1. Boundaries. What's okay in a discussion and what's not? How do you set a boundary when you realize you're knee-deep in BS?

2. Reliability. Bullshitting is the abandonment of reliability. It's hard to trust or be trusted when we BS too often.

3. Accountability. How do we hold ourself and others accountable for less BS and more honest debate? Less off-loading of emotion and more civility?

4. Vault. Civility honors confidentiality. BS ignores truth and opens the door to violations of confidentiality.

5. Integrity. How do we stay in our integrity when confronted with BS, and how do we stop in the midst of our own emotional moment to say, "You know what, I'm not sure this conversation is productive" or "I need to learn more about this issue"?

6. Nonjudgment. How do we stay out of judgment toward ourselves when the right thing to do is say, "I actually don't know much about this. Tell me what you know and why it's important to you." How do we not go into "winner/loser" mode and instead see an opportunity for connection when someone says to us, "I don't know anything about that issue"?

7. Generosity. What's the most generous assumption we can make about the people around us? What boundaries have to be in place for us to be kinder and more tolerant?

I know that the practice of speaking truth to bullshit while being civil feels like a paradox, but both are profoundly important parts of true belonging. Carl Jung wrote,

"Only the paradox comes anywhere near to comprehending the fullness of life." We are complex beings who wake up every day and fight against being labeled and diminished with stereotypes and characterizations that don't reflect our fullness. Yet when we don't risk standing on our own and speaking out, when the options laid before us force us into the very categories we resist, we perpetuate our own disconnection and loneliness. When we are willing to risk venturing into the wilderness, and even becoming our own wilderness, we feel the deepest connection to our true self and to what matters the most.

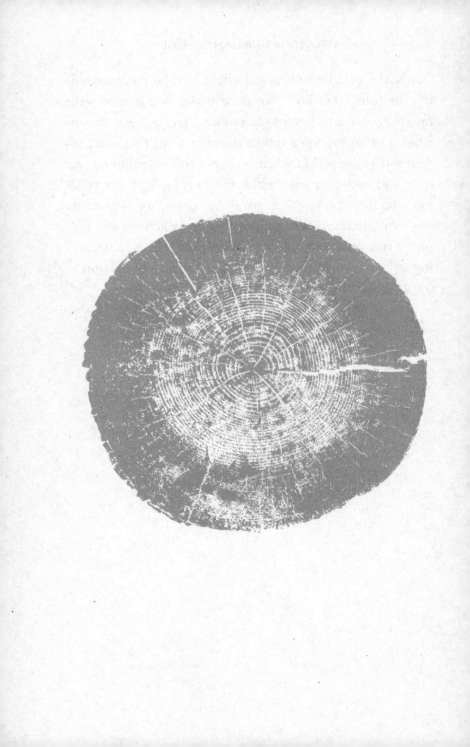

SIX

Hold Hands. With Strangers.

W e're in a spiritual crisis, and the key to building a true belonging practice is maintaining our belief in inextricable human connection. That connection—the spirit that flows between us and every other human in the world—is not something that can be broken; however, *our belief in the connection* is constantly tested and repeatedly severed. When our belief that there's something greater than us, something rooted in love and compassion, breaks, we are more likely to retreat to our bunkers, to hate from afar, to tolerate bullshit, to dehumanize others, and, ironically, to stay out of the wilderness.

It's counterintuitive, but our belief in inextricable human connection is one of our most renewable sources of courage in the wilderness. I can stand up for what I believe is right when I know that regardless of the pushback and criticism, I'm connected to myself and others in a way that can't be severed. When we don't believe in an unbreakable connection, the isolation of the wilderness is too daunting so we stay in our factions and echo chambers.

As hard as things are in the world right now, it's not just our polarizing culture that weakens our belief in inextricable human connection and strains our spiritual commitment to one another. It's also navigating the demands of our everyday lives. People are wonderful. *And* they can be hard. My favorite *Peanuts* cartoon is Linus crying "I love mankind . . . it's *people* I can't stand!" Everyday life can be incredibly hard, and the people around us can push us to the very edge of our nerves and our civility.

COVER IT ALL IN LEATHER

I love Pema Chödrön's "Lousy World" teaching on this topic. In it, Chödrön uses the lessons of the Indian Buddhist monk Shantideva to make a very powerful analogy about moving through the world constantly pissed off and disappointed. It's from a video, so I transcribed and edited her talk into something readable for us. Brace yourself. It's both familiar and uncomfortably true.

Chödrön starts:

This lousy world, these lousy people, this lousy government, this lousy everything . . . lousy weather . . . lousy blah, blah, blah. We're pissed off. It's too hot in here. It's too cold. I don't like the smell. The person in front is too tall and the person next to me is too fat.

That person is wearing perfume and I'm allergic to it . . . and just . . . *ugh!*

It's like being barefooted and walking across blazing-hot sand or across cut glass, or in a field with thorns. Your feet are bare and you say, "This is just too hard. It's really hurting, it's terrible, it's too sharp, it's too painful . . . it's too hot." But you have a great idea! You're just going to cover everywhere you go with leather. And then it won't hurt your feet anymore.

Spreading leather everywhere you go so you can cover the pain is like saying, "I'm going to get rid of her and get rid of him. I'm going to get the temperature right, and I'm going to ban perfume in the world, and then there will be nothing that bothers me anywhere. I am going to get rid of everything, including mosquitoes, that bothers me, anywhere in the world, and then I will be a very happy, content person."

[She pauses.]

We're laughing, but it's what we all do. That is how we approach things. We think, if we could just get rid of everything or cover it with leather, our pain would go away. Well, sure, because then it wouldn't be cutting our feet anymore. It's just logical, isn't it? But it doesn't make any sense, really. Shantideva said, "But if you simply wrap the leather around your feet." In other words, if you put on shoes then you could walk across the boiling sand and the cut glass and the thorns, and it wouldn't bother you. So the analogy is, if you work with your mind, instead of trying to change everything on the outside, that's how your temper will cool down.

So if we love the idea of humankind but people in general are constantly on our nerves, and we can't cover everything we don't like in leather, how do we cultivate and grow our belief in inextricable human connection internally? The answer that emerged from my research shocked me. *Show up for collective moments of joy and pain so we can actually bear witness to inextricable human connection.* Women and men with the strongest true belonging practices maintain their belief in inextricable connection by engaging in moments of joy and pain with strangers. In simpler terms, we have to catch some of that lightning in a bottle. We have to catch enough glimpses of people connecting to one another and having fun together that we believe it's true and possible for all of us.

Although catching these glimpses of human connection was a foreign research concept to me, I had more fun digging into what this means and what it looks like than I've had with almost any other work I've done in my career. And as I got my head around what this practice looks like in real life, I learned that I'm actually pretty good at it. Before this work, I didn't know why I put so much value on these collective moments. Why I intentionally go to a church where I can break bread, pass the peace, and sing with people who believe differently than I do, and people who I often want to punch in the arm. Why I cried the first time I took my kids to see U2 in concert and why they both reached out and held my hand during my favorite songs. Why the University of Texas fight song always makes me cheer and throw my "Hook 'em" sign up. Or why I've taught my kids that attending funerals is critically important, and when you're there, you show up. You take part. Every song. Every prayer—even if it's a language you don't understand or a faith you don't practice.

I always knew these moments were important to me. I knew they were connected to my spiritual well-being and allowed me to stay in love with humanity while doing research that can be devastating and hard. I just didn't know why. Now I do. Let's explore what experiences of collective joy and pain look like.

You'll Never Walk Alone

A couple of years ago, I clicked on a tweet by TED owner and curator Chris Anderson that read:

> When football = religion. Spine-tingling Aussie rendition of You'll Never Walk Alone.

The link took me to a YouTube video of ninety-five thousand Australian fans of the Liverpool Football Club gathered at the Melbourne Cricket Ground for a soccer match. For two minutes, I watched a stadium of Liverpool fans sway in unison as they sang the club's famous anthem, red scarves held high over their heads and tears streaming down many of their faces.

I was surprised to find myself fighting back my own tears. And based on the video's six million views, you can be sure that it wasn't just Liverpool fans, or even soccer fans, that found themselves misty-eyed and covered in goose-bumps. In fact, the first comment on YouTube was from a user with the handle "Manchester United Fan Prez"—Manchester being one of Liverpool's greatest rivals. The comment simply read: RESPECT.

Regardless of which team we're rooting for, the power of collective joy can transcend that division.

The next day, Steve and I made a commitment to make more time for football games (of the Texas variety), live music, and plays. In the age of YouTube, I'd started to forget what those moments felt like. And being there in person is so much more powerful.

CALLIN' BATON ROUGE

If you're within ten years on either side of my age and you grew up in the Texas I know, two names will bring a smile to your face and open up a flood of memories: George Strait and Garth Brooks. When my sisters, Ashley and Barrett, and I reminisce about growing up—our ex-boyfriends, our best moments, our worst moments, jeans that were so tight you had to use pliers to zip them up, and hair that reached for the sky—Garth Brooks and George Strait provide the sound-track. Every story has a song, and every song has a story.

Last year, Steve, Ashley, Barrett, Frankie (Barrett's husband), and I met our dear friends Rondal and Miles in San Antonio to see Garth Brooks and Trisha Year-wood in concert. It was extra fun because Rondal had worked with Garth for years, so we got to meet Garth and Trisha before the concert, who are as warm and down-home as you'd imagine. The concert was amazing—we knew the words to every song, and anyone who has ever seen Garth in concert will tell you that he's one helluva showman. The best moment for us was when he sang our collective favorite, "Callin' Baton Rouge." We didn't know it at the time, but Rondal had videotaped us through the entire thing. I still cry when I watch it.

Three or four months later, I was in the car with my sisters and my nieces when I turned to Barrett and said, "Let's listen to 'Baton Rouge'!"

Gabi, Barrett's six-year-old daughter, said, "No! I want to listen to 'Number 1'! I want to listen to the one we sing to every day."

Barrett laughed. " 'Baton Rouge' *is* 'Number 1.' "

My sisters and I confessed we had been listening to that song on repeat since the concert. All three of us had owned the CD that included the song before the concert, but only after that moment of joy and connection did we start listening to it three times a day, every day. So what was happening? That song took us back to a moment. If you watch it on Rondal's video, it is a moment you can only describe as pure love: love for music, for our history together, and for one another. All three of us are hugging and holding hands and sing-screaming the words at the top of our lungs:

Operator, won't you put me on through
I gotta send my love down to Baton Rouge.

Wands Up

It's no secret that I'm a Harry Potter fan. My daughter, Ellen, grew up with the books, and we were always among the first in line for book and movie releases. In 2009 we attended opening night for *Harry Potter and the Half-Blood Prince*. There were plenty of Gryffindor scarves, forehead scars sketched out of eyeliner, and T-shirts that read KEEP CALM AND CARRY A WAND in evidence.

SPOILER ALERT: Sadly, toward the end of the film, our wise guide and faithful leader Dumbledore is killed. There's a scene where Harry is bent over his body, weeping. Dumbledore was the headmaster of the Hogwarts school and a father figure, mentor, and protector to Harry. Even if you've never read the books or seen the movies, you know the scene: a young protagonist losing his or her parent figure and guide. It's an essential element in the arc of many great stories and a pivotal part of what Joseph Campbell called the Hero's Journey.

As a crowd of students and professors gathers around Dumbledore's body, an evil face appears in the dark sky. It is the face of Voldemort, the person responsible for Dumbledore's death. As Harry places a hand on Dumbledore's chest and continues to weep, Dumbledore's dearest friend and fellow teacher, Professor McGonagall, played brilliantly by Dame Maggie Smith, raises her wand to the sky. From the tip of the wand comes a single burst of light. One by one, each student and teacher raises his or her wand to create a constellation of light that overcomes the dark and menacing sky.

At that moment in a movie theater in Houston, a universe away from Hogwarts School of Witchcraft and Wizardry, I looked around to find that two hundred strangers, most of them with tears on their cheeks, had their hands in the air, pointing their imaginary wands to the sky. Why? Because we believe in the light. Yes, we know that Harry Potter is not real, but we know that collective light *is* real. And powerful. And in the face of hatred and bigotry and cruelty and everything that dark sky stood for, we were so much stronger together.

The People of FM 1960

I know exactly where I was on January 28, 1986. I was in Houston driving down FM 1960, a busy four-lane thoroughfare close to the suburb of Klein, where I lived when I was in high school. I remember I was driving through an intersection when I saw cars suddenly pulling over to the curb. A few actually stopped right in the middle of their lane. My first thought was that a fire truck or ambulance must be coming from behind us. I slowed down to a crawl, but even after I checked over and over—in my side mirror, in my rearview mirror, craning my neck to look behind me—I couldn't see the lights of an emergency vehicle.

As I slowly rolled past a pickup truck that was pulled over to the curb, I glanced inside the cab of the truck and saw a man leaning on his steering wheel with his head buried in his hands. I immediately thought, *We're at war.* I pulled over in front of him and turned on the radio just in time to hear the announcer say, "Again, the space shuttle *Challenger* has exploded."

No. No. No. No. I started crying. I saw more people pulling over. Some were even getting out of their cars. It was as if people were desperate to bear witness to this tragedy with others—to not have to know this alone.

NASA is not just a beacon of possibility in space exploration for us in Houston—it's where our friends and neighbors work. These are our people. Christa McAuliffe was going to be the first teacher in space. Teachers everywhere are our people.

After five or ten minutes, people started driving again. But now as they slowly made their way back into normal traffic, they had their headlights on. No one on the radio said, "Turn your lights on if you're driving." Somehow we instinctively knew that we were all part of this procession of grief. I didn't know those people or even talk to them, but if you ask where I was when the *Challenger* disaster happened, I will say, "I was with my people—the people of FM 1960—when that tragedy occurred."

WE CHOOSE LOVE

Our kids were first graders. Their kids were first graders. The pain, horror, and fear were unfathomable. We gathered for no other reason than to be with one another. We didn't come together to make sense of what had happened in that school so far away from our own because we never,

ever wanted it to make sense. We sat crying in silence, our small group of neighborhood mothers, some friends and some strangers, who had felt compelled to be together. It was December 15, 2012, the day after twenty-year-old Adam Lanza fatally shot twenty children between six and seven years old, as well as six adult staff members, at Sandy Hook Elementary School in Newtown, Connecticut.

I remember thinking, *Maybe if all the mothers in the world crawled on their hands and knees toward those parents in Newtown, we could take some of the pain away. We could spread their pain across all of our hearts. I would do it. Can't we find a way to hold some of it for them? I'll take my share. Even if it adds sadness to all my days.*

My friends and I didn't rush to start a fund that day. We didn't storm the principal's office at our kids' school asking for increased security measures. We didn't call politicians or post on Facebook. We would do all that in the days to come. But the day right after the shooting, we just sat together with nothing but the sound of occasional weeping cutting through the silence. Leaning in to our shared pain and fear comforted us.

Being alone in the midst of a widely reported trauma, watching endless hours of twenty-four-hour news or reading countless articles on the Internet, is the quickest way for anxiety and fear to tiptoe into your heart and plant their roots of secondary trauma. That day after the mass killing, I chose to cry with my friends, then I headed to church to cry with strangers.

I couldn't have known then that in 2017 I would speak

at a fund-raiser for the Resiliency Center of Newtown and spend time sitting with a group of parents whose children were killed at Sandy Hook. What I've learned through my work and what I heard that night in Newtown makes one thing clear: Not enough of us know how to sit in pain with others. Worse, our discomfort shows up in ways that can hurt people and reinforce their own isolation. I have started to believe that crying with strangers in person could save the world.

Today there's a sign that welcomes you to Newtown: WE ARE SANDY HOOK. WE CHOOSE LOVE. That day when I sat in a room with other mothers from my neighborhood and cried, I wasn't sure what we were doing or why. Today I'm pretty sure we were choosing love in our own small way.

INEXTRICABLE CONNECTION

All of these examples of collective joy and pain are sacred experiences. They are so deeply human that they cut through our differences and tap into our hardwired nature. These experiences tell us what is true and possible about the human spirit. We need these moments with strangers as reminders that despite how much we might dislike someone on Facebook or even in person, we are still inextricably connected. And it doesn't have to be a big moment with thousands of strangers. We can be reminded of our inextricable connection after talking with a seatmate on a two-hour flight.

The problem is that we don't show up for enough of these experiences. We clearly need them. But it's vulnerable to lean in to that kind of shared joy and pain. We armor up. We shove our hands into our pockets during the concert or we roll our eyes at the dance or put our headphones on rather than get to know someone on the train.

Here's why we need to catch these moments of human spark and be grateful for them: Walk onto the pitch in Melbourne and ask the audience to stop singing the Liverpool anthem and start talking about Brexit, you've got a problem. Turn on the lights in the theater and ask the Harry Potter fans and their parents to discuss the pros and cons of public schools versus private schools versus homeschooling, Voldemort will look friendly.

If you gathered the men and women of FM 1960 in a room away from the time and context of the *Challenger* tragedy and asked them whether the U.S. government should put more money into defense spending, social welfare programs, or space exploration, do you think you'd see a lot of random hugging and patting on the back? Turn the Garth Brooks concert into a political rally, and it's likely you'll see singing turn into a screaming match. All of these scenarios will more than likely fuel disconnection and reinforce assumptions that we are nothing alike.

But the more we're willing to seek out moments of collective joy and show up for experiences of collective pain— for real, in person, not online—the more difficult it becomes to deny our human connection, even with people we may disagree with. Not only do moments of collective emotion remind us of what is possible between people, but they also remind us of what is true about the human spirit.

We are wired for connection. But the key is that, in any given moment of it, it has to be real.

A SENSATION OF SACREDNESS

The French sociologist Émile Durkheim introduced the term *collective effervescence* in his 1912 book *The Elementary Forms of the Religious Life*. Durkheim was investigating what he originally described as a type of magic that he witnessed during religious ceremonies. Durkheim explained that collective effervescence is an experience of connection, communal emotion, and a "sensation of sacredness" that happens when we are a part of something bigger than us. Durkheim also proposed that during these experiences of collective effervescence our focus shifts from self to group.

Researchers Shira Gabriel, Jennifer Valenti, Kristin Naragon-Gainey, and Ariana Young recently developed and validated an instrument to measure how experiences of *collective assembly* (their term for these experiences) affect us. They found that these experiences contribute to a life filled with "a sense of meaning, increased positive affect, an increased sense of social connection, and a decreased sense of loneliness—all essential components of a healthy, happy life."

In their 2017 paper, they write, "It is consistent with the idea that collective assembly is more than just people coming together to distract themselves from life by watching a game, concert, or play—instead it is an opportunity to feel connected to something bigger than oneself; it is an opportunity to feel joy, social connection, meaning, and peace.

Collective assembly has long been a part of the human experience and the current work begins to quantify its important psychological benefits." And there seems to be a lingering effect—we hold on to our feelings of social connectedness and well-being past the actual event.

I loved discovering that the study's lead researcher, Shira Gabriel, first learned about collective effervescence through her own experiences following the band Phish through grad school. My younger brother is a Deadhead who also followed Phish around, so I totally connected with her story. Gabriel and her research team have tapped into why customs, pilgrimages, and feast days played such an important part in early religious culture, and why today we still love to gather at protests, sporting events, and concerts. We want more meaning and connection in our lives.

In the interviews with our own research participants, music emerged as one of the most powerful conveners of collective joy and pain. It's often at the heart of spiritual gatherings, celebrations, funerals, and protest movements. Ever since 2012, when I led an audience of a thousand people at the World Domination Summit in Portland in a Journey sing-along, I've never doubted the power of music as the most powerful form of collective joy. I still get emails from people who were there that day. One of the recent emails captured the sentiments shared by most of the people who reached out to me after that event: "I've tried to explain what it was like to be there that day, but you just can't put the experience into words. It was magic."

A MINISTRY OF PRESENCE

Only holiness will call people to listen now. And the work of holiness is not about perfection or niceness; it is about belonging, that sense of being in the Presence and through the quality of that belonging, the mild magnetic of implicating others in the Presence. . . . This is not about forging a relationship with a distant God but about the realization that we are already within God.

—JOHN O'DONOHUE

Just recently I found myself in the overflow room of a church in a small Texas town. I was at the funeral for my good friend Laura's father. There were no choir members or pianos in the overflow room, just a few hundred people in folding chairs watching the eulogies in the main church via a projector and computer screen. When we were asked to stand and sing one of his (and my) favorite hymns, "How Great Thou Art," I wasn't so sure how two hundred or so strangers could pull off singing an old hymn a cappella in a reception hall. But we did, and it was a holy experience.

Laura's dad was a small-town hero who never met a stranger. All I could think in that moment was, *He would have loved our messy voices and singing hearts.* The neurologist Oliver Sacks writes, "Music, uniquely among the arts, is both completely abstract and profoundly emotional. . . . Music can pierce the heart directly; it needs no mediation."

Funerals, in fact, are one of the most powerful examples of collective pain. They feature in a surprising finding from my research on trust. When I asked participants to identify three to five specific behaviors that their friends, family, and colleagues do that raise their level of trust with them, funerals always emerged in the top three responses. Funerals matter. Showing up to them matters. And funerals matter not just to the people grieving, but to everyone who is there. The collective pain (and sometimes joy) we experience when gathering in any way to celebrate the end of a life is perhaps one of the most powerful experiences of inextricable connection. Death, loss, and grief are the great equalizers.

My aunt Betty died while I was writing this book. When I think of her I think of laughing, camping, swimming in the Nueces River, driving to her ranch in Hondo, Texas, and our silent agreement that we would never discuss politics. I also think of the time when I was about seven years old and I begged her to let me go into the "card room" where the parents, grandparents, and oldest cousins were yelling, laughing, cussing, smoking, and playing Rook (our family's favorite card game). I was stuck in the "kids' room," which was so boring. She held my cheeks in her hand and said, "I can't let you go in there. Plus, trust me, you don't want to see what's in there. It ain't pretty."

Rather than holding a funeral, it was Betty's wish that we come together for a family barbecue potluck in my cousin Danny's backyard. She just wanted us to laugh and be together. Danny led us in prayer, we told funny stories, and Nathan played the guitar while Diana sang the "Ave Maria." It was 90 degrees in the Texas Hill Country and you could barely hear the stories and music over the shrilling of the cicadas. I kept thinking, *This is exactly what it means to be human.*

This humanity transcends all of those differences that keep up us apart. In Sheryl Sandberg and Adam Grant's beautiful 2017 book about grief and courage, *Option B*, Sandberg tells a wrenching and wholehearted story about collective pain. Her husband, Dave, died suddenly while they were on vacation. Their children were in second and fourth grade. She writes, "When we arrived at the cemetery, my children got out of the car and fell to the ground, unable to take another step. I lay on the grass, holding them as they wailed. Their cousins came and lay down with us, all piled up in a big sobbing heap with adult arms trying in vain to protect them from their sorrow."

Sandberg told her children, "This is the second worst moment of our lives. We lived through the first and we will live through this. It can only get better from here." She then started singing a song she knew from childhood, "Oseh Shalom," a prayer for peace. She writes, "I don't remember deciding to sing or how I picked this song. I later learned that it is the last line of the Kaddish, the Jewish prayer for mourning, which may explain why it poured out of me. Soon all the adults joined in, the children followed, and the wailing stopped."

An experience of collective pain does not deliver us from grief or sadness; it is a ministry of presence. These moments remind us that we are not alone in our darkness and that our broken heart is connected to every heart that has known pain since the beginning of time.

COMMON ENEMY INTIMACY

I remember snort-laughing the first time I saw a pillow on my friend's sofa that said IF YOU DON'T HAVE ANYTHING NICE TO SAY, COME SIT NEXT TO ME. Let me take the researcher-trying-to-be-a-good-person hat off for a minute and ask a couple of honest questions: Is there a faster, easier way to make friends with a stranger than to talk smack about someone you both know? Is there anything better than the feeling of plopping down next to someone and getting really snarky, gossipy, and judgmental? Of course in both cases I often feel like total shit later—but let's be honest about how awesome it feels in the moment, right when it's happening. It is a seductive, reliable, and super easy way to connect with just about anyone. And oh my God, it can be funny.

But let's get to the flip side of that pillow. The connection that we forge by judging and mocking others is not real connection, like the examples I wrote about above. Yet, unfortunately, the pain it causes is real pain. A connection built on snark has about as much value as snark itself—nada.

When I was interviewing people for my shame research, many of the participants talked about the pain of overhearing people talking about them or the shame of learning what the "gossip" was about them. It was so heart-wrenching that I started working on a no-gossip practice. Damn, that was lonely at first. But it was also painfully educational. It was only a matter of weeks before I realized that several of my connections, what I thought of as real friendships, were founded entirely on talking about other people. Once that was gone, we had nothing in common and nothing to talk about.

If you zoom out from our personal lives to the political and ideological culture we live in today, I would argue that the people we're sitting next to on those snark couches are often not people with whom we feel inextricably connected or with whom we feel a deep sense of community. We've simply started hanging out with people who hate the same people we do. That's not connection. That's "you're either with us or against us." That's common enemy intimacy. *I don't really know you, nor am I invested in our relationship, but I do like that we hate the same people and have contempt for the same ideas.*

Common enemy intimacy is counterfeit connection and the opposite of true belonging. If the bond we share with others is simply that we hate the same people, the intimacy we experience is often intense, immediately gratifying, and an easy way to discharge outrage and pain. It is not, however, fuel for real connection. It's fuel that runs hot, burns fast, and leaves a trail of polluted emotion. And if we live with any level of self-awareness, it's also the kind of intimacy that can leave us with the intense regrets of an integrity hangover. *Did I really participate in that? Is that moving us forward? Am I engaging in, quite literally, the exact same behavior that I find loathsome in others?*

I get that these are uncertain and threatening times. I often feel the pull of hiding out and finding safety with a crew. But it's not working. While we may all be gathered behind the same bunkers of political or social belief and ideology, we're still alone in them. And even worse, we're constantly monitoring ourselves. The looming threat of blowback should we voice an opinion or idea that challenges our bunker mates keeps us anxious. When all that binds us is what we believe rather than who we are, changing our mind or challenging the collective ideology is risky.

When a group or community doesn't tolerate dissent and disagreement, it forgoes any experience of inextricable connection. There is no true belonging, only an unspoken treaty to hate the same people. This fuels our spiritual crisis of disconnection.

So just as profoundly as collective experiences move us, it is clear that not all of these moments are created equal. When a collective comes together at the expense of others—for example, to bond over the devaluation or debasing of another person or group of people, or to bond despite this—it does not heal the spiritual crisis of disconnection. In fact, it does quite the opposite by feeding it. It is not true collective joy if it's at the expense of others, and it is not true collective pain if it causes others pain. When soccer fans yell racist taunts at players or when people gather in hate for any reason, the practices of true belonging and inextricable connection are immediately voided and bankrupted.

When I asked research participants about protest marches and gatherings as experiences of collective joy and/or pain, the responses were the same as when I asked about religious services: "It depends on the experience." As I dug in to better understand why some were and some were not, the dividing lines that develop around common enemy intimacy resurfaced: Dehumanizing and objectifying negate collective joy and pain. A woman in her mid-forties explained, "I can go to church and have the most amazing experience of spiritual connection. I feel part of something that transcends difference. I can also go to church and leave feeling enraged after my priest uses the homily for a platform to talk about politics and endorse candidates. Those experiences are becoming more and more common. At some point it won't be worth going back."

My daughter and I participated in the 2017 Women's March in Washington, D.C. For me, some moments felt like true collective joy *and* pain, and other moments fell outside that experience. Due to an unfortunate Uber drop-off, we got caught in some of the scary and senseless property destruction at the edges of the march and the ensuing riot police activity. That was quickly followed by two young guys in Trump hats screaming "Fuck you, libtards!" at a group of young women who were just walking down the street in their feminist T-shirts.

Within a one-block walk we had visible proof that extremists at both ends of the political continuum have more in common with each other than they do with the vast majority of people from their own constituencies. What they share is leveraging any opportunity to discharge their denied and festering pain, hurt, and feelings of smallness or powerlessness. Again, those emotions will not be denied and when we work them out on people, it's dangerous.

Most of the speakers at the march brought us together in moments of unity, but a few exploited emotion in ways very similar to the tactics of the people they were railing against, including dehumanizing comments about politicians. What I found interesting was how you could physically feel the energy shifting from the crowd to the speaker in those moments that took us from "Here's what's possible!" and "Here's what we believe in!" to "Here's what and who we hate." The energy shifted from the power of the people to the performance of the speaker.

Collective assembly meets the primal human yearnings for shared social experiences. We need to be mindful, however, of how and when those yearnings are being exploited and manipulated for purposes other than authentic connection. One collective assembly can start to heal the wounds of a traumatized community, while another can initiate trauma in that same community. When we come together to share authentic joy, hope, and pain, we melt the pervasive cynicism that often cloaks our better human nature. When we come together under the false flag of common enemy intimacy, we amplify cynicism and diminish our collective worth.

GETTING SOCIAL

In our efforts to create more opportunities for collective joy and pain, can social media play a positive role, or have they just become a home for hate and cat pictures? Can social media help us develop real relationships and true belonging, or do they always get in the way? These are the questions that all of us are wrestling with today.

There are days when I love everything about social media, from the swift and powerful justice they can deliver to the endless stream of pictures of cupcakes decorated to look like succulents. Then there are days when I'm sure that Facebook, Twitter, and Instagram exist solely to piss me off, hurt my feelings, remind me of my inadequacies, and give dangerous people a platform.

I've come to the conclusion that the way we engage with social media is like fire—you can use them to keep yourself warm and nourished, or you can burn down the barn. It all depends on your intentions, expectations, and reality-checking skills.

As I started digging into this question with research participants, there was very little ambiguity. It became clear that face-to-face connection is imperative in our true belonging practice. Not only did face-to-face contact emerge as essential from the participant data in my research, but studies across the world confirm those findings. Social media are helpful in cultivating connection only to the extent that they're used to create real community where there is structure, purpose, and meaning, and some face-to-face contact.

One of the most well-respected researchers in this area is Susan Pinker. In her book *The Village Effect: How Face-to-Face Contact Can Make Us Healthier and Happier*, Pinker writes, "In a short evolutionary time, we have changed from group-living primates skilled at reading each other's every gesture and intention to a solitary species, each one of us preoccupied with our own screen." Based on studies across diverse fields, Pinker concludes that there is no substitute for in-person interactions. They are proven to bolster our immune system, send positive hormones surging through our bloodstream and brain, and help us live longer. Pinker adds, "I call this building your village, and building it is a matter of life or death."

When she says "life or death," she's not kidding. It turns out that everything she's learned complements what we read about loneliness: Social interaction makes us live longer, healthier lives. By a lot. Pinker writes, "In fact, neglecting to keep in close contact with people who are important to you is at least as dangerous to your health as a pack-a-day cigarette habit, hypertension, or obesity."

The good news is that this contact doesn't have to be a long, close interaction, though that's nice. Making eye contact, shaking someone's hand, or giving someone a high-five lowers your cortisone level and releases dopamine, making you less stressed and providing a little chemical boost. Pinker writes, "Research shows that playing cards once a week or meeting friends every Wednesday night at Starbucks adds as many years to our lives as taking beta blockers or quitting a pack-a-day smoking habit."

Social media are great for developing community, but for true belonging, real connection and real empathy require meeting real people in a real space in real time. I have an example of this from my own life.

FACEBOOK AND MY FIRST TRUE LOVE

Remember Eleanor from chapter 1, my BFF during my family's stint in New Orleans? She was my best friend in the whole world. We met when we were five years old. First best friends are really first true loves. She was mine and I was hers. For years we were inseparable. Every day during the school year, we would ride our bikes through the Tulane campus to and from school, sometimes stopping to get ice cream or sneak into Der Rathskeller at the student union for a soda.

We had an entire dance and lip-sync routine to "Band on the Run" by Paul McCartney and Wings. We cut up during Mass and prided ourselves on never getting caught. One day we snuck into the back of the Newman Center, where we'd often attend what we lovingly called "hippie church," and ate a handful of communion wafers. We were sure we'd go straight to hell, but at least we'd be together. We both came from big families, so we loved nothing more than escaping the fray by going out together on our bikes for shenanigans.

As I wrote earlier, when I was in fourth grade, my dad got transferred from New Orleans to Houston. Eleanor and I were devastated. But we made a pact to make the best of it and visit each other when we could. In advance of the move, my parents took me out of school for a week and dropped my brother, my sisters, and me off at my grandmother's house in San Antonio while they went house hunting in Houston. I was nine, Jason was five, and the twins were one.

We weren't at my grandmother's house more than a day before both twins got a stomach bug. Then I got sick. Then my brother got sick. My grandmother waved off my parents when they called from Houston and insisted she could hold down the fort. Two days, five trips to the laundromat, and one gallon of chicken soup later, everyone was better but me. I was getting sicker. I finally got so sick that my grandmother told my parents to come back.

Within twenty-four hours, I was in emergency surgery for a ruptured and gangrenous appendix. My grandmother had no way of knowing; it was just the perfect storm of nearly identical symptoms. Problems soon multiplied. There was some question as to whether the surgeon called in for the emergency surgery had been completely sober, and immediate post-operation complications developed. Eventually my parents wheeled me out "against medical advice" in the middle of the night to another hospital, where I spent two weeks recovering. My parents then left me in Texas with my grandmother when they went back to pack up the house.

I never saw Eleanor again.

But in early 2009, I found Eleanor on Facebook. I reached out and within minutes we reconnected (*thank you, Facebook!*). Since then our families have spent time together. I'm close to her kids, she's close to mine, and our husbands are friends. It has truly been one of the most unexpected joys of my life. The first time we were together again we spent hours downloading everything, from the pain and loss we'd survived over the years to our most searing moments of happiness. It was a conversation that could have never happened online. It needed a couch in the middle of the night, tea, and pajamas.

The point I want to make is that the joy didn't come

from reconnecting on Facebook. It came and still comes from our long walks, family Ping-Pong and four square tournaments, and watching movies together. Facebook was the catalyst. Face-to-face was the connection.

COURAGE AND THE COLLECTIVE

One of the things I love to do when I teach the concept of vulnerability is to show students videos of flash mobs and other moments of collective joy. What you'll see in all these videos is the way school-aged children unapologetically and wholeheartedly lean in to the experience. Adults? Some yes and some not so much. Tweens and teens? Rarely. They're more likely to be mortified. Both joy and pain are vulnerable experiences to feel on our own and even more so with strangers.

The foundation of courage is vulnerability—the ability to navigate uncertainty, risk, and emotional exposure. It takes courage to open ourselves up to joy. In fact, as I've written in other books, I believe joy is probably the most vulnerable emotion we experience. We're afraid that if we allow ourselves to feel it, we'll get blindsided by disaster or disappointment. That's why in moments of real joy, many of us dress-rehearse tragedy. We see our child leave for the prom, and all we can think is "car crash." We get excited about an upcoming vacation, and we start thinking "hurricane." We try to beat vulnerability to the punch by imagining the worst or by feeling nothing in hopes that the "other shoe won't drop." I call it foreboding joy.

The only way to combat foreboding joy is gratitude. Across the years, the men and women who could most fully lean in to joy were those who practiced gratitude. In those vulnerable moments of individual or collective joy, we need to practice gratitude.

Pain is also a vulnerable emotion. It takes real courage to allow ourselves to feel pain. When we're suffering, many of us are better at causing pain than feeling it. We spread hurt rather than let it inside.

So, to seek out moments of collective joy and to show up for moments of collective pain, we have to be brave. That means we have to be vulnerable. In all my research's two-hundred-thousand-plus pieces of data, I can't find a single example of courage that didn't require vulnerability. Can you, in your life? Can you think of one moment of courage that didn't require risk, uncertainty, and emotional exposure? I know the answer is no; I've asked too many people who say this—including special operations soldiers. No vulnerability, no courage. We have to show up and put ourselves out there. When the singing starts and the dancing is under way, at the very least we need to tap our toes and hum along. When the tears fall and the hard story is shared, we have to show up and stay with the pain.

And as much as we value "going it alone" and as much as we sometimes gather together for the wrong reasons, in our hearts we want to believe that despite our differences and despite the need to brave the wilderness, we don't always have to walk alone.

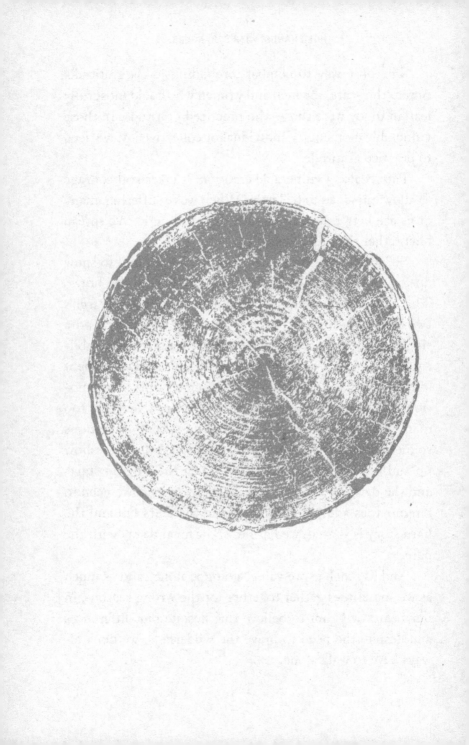

SEVEN

Strong Back. Soft Front. Wild Heart.

All too often our so-called strength comes from fear, not love;
instead of having a strong back, many of us have a defended
front shielding a weak spine. In other words, we walk around
brittle and defensive, trying to conceal our lack of confidence. If
we strengthen our backs, metaphorically speaking, and develop a
spine that's flexible but sturdy, then we can risk having a front
that's soft and open. . . . How can we give and accept care with
strong-back, soft-front compassion, moving past fear into a place
of genuine tenderness? I believe it comes about when we can be
truly transparent, seeing the world clearly—
and letting the world see into us.
—ROSHI JOAN HALIFAX

The first time I heard the term "strong back, soft front" was from Joan Halifax. We were doing an event together at the Omega Institute in New York—one of my favorite places. I'll admit that I was a little intimidated to meet her; Dr. Halifax is a Buddhist teacher, Zen priest, anthropologist, activist, and author of several books on Engaged Buddhism. We met for the first time during the technical rehearsal for our evening talk. She was down-to-earth and, what I remember most, she was funny as hell. As we were leaving I said, "I'm wiped, but I guess it's off to the meet-and-greet."

She looked at me and said, "I'm going to my room to rest before tonight. Why don't you do the same?"

I told her that sounded great, but I felt bad saying no. I'll never forget what she said back to me. "Tonight we will exhale and teach. Now it's time to inhale. There is the in-breath and there is the out-breath, and it's easy to believe that we must exhale all the time, without ever inhaling. But the inhale is absolutely essential if you want to continue to exhale."

Dang.

During her talk that night she explained the Buddhist approach of strong back, soft front. As I was working through the research on this book, this image kept coming back to me. If we're going to make true belonging a daily practice in our lives, we're going to need a strong back and a soft front. We'll need both courage and vulnerability as we abandon the certainty and safety of our ideological bunkers and head off into the wilderness.

True belonging is, however, more than strong back and soft front. Once we've found the courage to stand alone, to say what we believe and do what we feel is right despite the criticism and fear, we may leave the wilderness, but the wild has marked our hearts. That doesn't mean the wilderness is no longer difficult, it means that once we've braved it on our own, we will be painfully aware of our choices moving forward. We can spend our entire life betraying ourself and choosing fitting in over standing alone. But once we've stood up for ourself and our beliefs, the bar is higher. A wild heart fights fitting in and grieves betrayal.

STRONG BACK

All of us will spend our life constantly strengthening our back, softening our front, and trying to listen to the whispers of our wild heart. For some of us, however, the focus of our work will be on developing that strong back. When strengthening our back is our particular challenge, we are often driven by what people think. Perfecting, pleasing, proving, and pretending get in the way of the strong back. One way to strengthen our courage muscle is learning how to put BRAVING into practice. That work looks like this:

Boundaries: Learning to set, hold, and respect boundaries. The challenge is letting go of being liked and the fear of disappointing people.

Reliability: Learning how to say what we mean and mean what we say. The challenge is not overcommitting and overpromising to please others or prove ourselves.

Accountability: Learning how to step up, be accountable, take responsibility, and issue meaningful apologies when we're wrong. The challenge is letting go of blame and staying out of shame.

Vault: Learning how to keep confidences, to recognize what's ours to share and what's not. The challenge is to stop using gossip, common enemy intimacy, and oversharing as a way to hotwire connection.

Integrity: Learning how to practice our values even when it's uncomfortable and hard. The challenge is choosing courage over comfort in those moments.

Nonjudgment: Learning how to give and receive help. The challenge is letting go of "helper and fixer" as our identity and the source of our self-worth.

Generosity: Learning how to set the boundaries that allow us to be generous in our assumptions about others. The challenge is being honest and clear with others about what's okay and not okay.

In her interview with Bill Moyers, Dr. Angelou said, "I belong to myself. I am very proud of that. I am very concerned about how I look at Maya. I like Maya very much." Our work is to get to the place where we like ourselves and are concerned when we judge ourselves too harshly or allow others to silence us. The wilderness demands this level of self-love and self-respect.

A powerful example of a strong back comes from my friend Jen Hatmaker. Jen is a writer, pastor, philanthropist, and community leader. Last year I watched her navigate a brutal wilderness with grace, grief, and strength. As a well-known religious leader in a conservative-to-moderate Christian community, Jen wrote openly about her support of LGBTQ rights and inclusion. She experienced an openly hostile response from many in her community. I asked her about what that wilderness looked and felt like to her. Here's what she wrote:

I won't sugarcoat this: Standing on the precipice of the wilderness is bone-chilling. Because belonging is so primal, so necessary, the threat of losing your tribe or going alone feels so terrifying as to keep most of us distanced from the wilderness our whole lives. Human approval is one of our most treasured idols, and the offering we must lay at its hungry feet is *keeping others comfortable*. I'm convinced that discomfort is the great deterrent of our generation. Protecting the status quo against our internal convictions is obviously a luxury of the privileged, because the underdogs and outliers and marginalized have no choice but to experience the daily wilderness. But choosing the wily outpost over the security of the city gates takes a true act of courage. That first step will take your breath away.

Speaking against power structures that keep some inside and others outside has a cost, and the currency most often drafted from my account is *belonging*. Consequently, the wilderness sometimes feels very lonely and punishing, which is a powerful disincentive. But I've discovered something beautiful; the loneliest steps are the ones between the city walls and the heart of the wilderness, where safety is in the rearview mirror, new territory remains to be seen, and the path out to the unknown seems empty. But put one foot in front of the other enough times, stay the course long enough to actually tunnel into the wilderness, and you'll be shocked how many people already live out there— thriving, dancing, creating, celebrating, belonging. It is not a barren wasteland. It is not unprotected territory. It is not void of human flourishing. The wilderness is where all the creatives and prophets and system-buckers and risk-takers have always lived, and it is stunningly vibrant. The walk out there is hard, but the authenticity out there is life.

I suspect the wilderness is a permanent home for me, which is both happy and hard. A dear friend sent me a text during those harsh first steps out, having broken party lines irreversibly after publicly wrestling through a fragile doctrinal interpretation. There is this wonderful and strange story in Genesis 32 about Jacob physically wrestling with God all night in the literal wilderness, and upon realizing that Jacob was positively not giving up and in fact hollered, *"I will not let you go unless you bless me!,"* he touched Jacob's hip and wrenched it out of socket, a permanent reminder of the struggle of a determined, stubborn, dogged man with God; an absurd and ballsy move, as outrageous as it was impressive. My friend texted me: *"You are like Jacob. You refused to let go of God until He blessed you in this space. And He will. You will indeed find new land. But you'll always walk with a limp."* So I've chosen the wilderness, because it is where I can tell the truth and lead with the most courage and gather with my fellow outsiders, but this limp will remind me of the cost, what lies behind me, what will always feel a little sad and a little bruised. Was it worth it? Unquestionably. And I hope the limp shows my fellow wilderness dwellers that I'm acquainted with pain and didn't make it out here unscathed either. Outliers, I suspect it won't hinder our wilderness dance party in the slightest.

A wilderness dance party? I'm in.

A SOFT FRONT

Jen's incredible story about her experiences in the wilderness drove home two points for me:

1. We have to maintain our strong back—it's not a one-time effort; and
2. Man, is it hard to keep the front soft when there's so much hurt.

Like Jen, I've shared opinions with my community and experienced pushback from some people that took my breath away. Everything from "Keep your mouth shut" to violent and graphic threats against my family. My visceral response is "Strong back, *armored* front." But that's no way to live. Vulnerability is the birthplace of love, joy, trust, intimacy, courage—everything that brings meaning to our life. An armored front sounds good when we're hurting but causes us much more pain in the end. When we let people take our vulnerability or fill us with their hate, we turn over our entire life to them.

Many of us armor up early as a way to protect ourself as children. Once we grow into adults, we start to realize that the armor is preventing us from growing into our gifts and ourself. Just like we can strengthen our courage muscle for a stronger back by examining our need to be perfect and please others at the expense of our own life, we can exercise the vulnerability muscle that allows us to soften and stay open rather than attack and defend. This means getting comfortable with vulnerability. Most of the time we approach life with an armored front for two reasons: 1) We're not comfortable with emotions and we equate vulnerability with weakness, and/or 2) Our experiences of trauma have taught us that vulnerability is actually dangerous. Violence and oppression have made our soft front a liability, and we struggle to find a place emotionally and physically safe enough to be vulnerable. The definition of vulnerability is uncertainty, risk, and emotional exposure. But vulnerability is not weakness; it's our most accurate measure of courage. When the barrier is our belief about vulnerability, the question becomes: *Are we willing to show up and be seen when we can't control the outcome?* When the barrier to vulnerability is about safety, the question becomes: *Are we willing to create courageous spaces so we can be fully seen?*

A soft and open front is not being weak; it's being brave, it's being the wilderness.

WILD HEART

I wish there was a secret handshake for the wild heart club. I love that kind of stuff. I want the payoff for braving the wilderness to be some kind of ritual or symbol that says, *I'm part of this wild heart club. I know what it means to stand alone and brave the criticism, fear, and hurt. I know the freedom of belonging everywhere and nowhere at all. The reward is great, but believe me, when Maya Angelou said "the price is high"—she was not kidding. I have made this quest and I have the scars to prove it.*

But the wilderness doesn't issue membership cards. A wild heart is not something you can always see—and yet it is our greatest spiritual possession. Remember Carl Jung's words about paradox: "The paradox is one of our most valuable spiritual possessions . . . only the paradox comes anywhere near to comprehending the fullness of life." Learning how to navigate the tension inherent in the four practices and the many paradoxes outlined in this book is a critical piece of addressing our current spiritual crisis.

The mark of a wild heart is living out the paradox of love in our lives. It's the ability to be tough and tender, excited and scared, brave and afraid—all in the same moment. It's showing up in our vulnerability and our courage, being both fierce and kind.

A wild heart can also straddle the tension of staying awake to the struggle in the world and fighting for justice and peace, while also cultivating its own moments of joy. I know a lot of people, myself included, who feel guilt and even shame about their own moments of joy. How can I play on this gorgeous beach with my family while there are people who have no home or safety? Why am I working so hard to decorate my son's birthday cupcakes like cute little *Despicable Me* minions when there are so many Syrian children starving to death? *What difference do these stupid cupcakes really make?* They matter because joy matters.

Whether you're a full-time activist or a volunteer at your mosque or local soup kitchen, most of us are showing up to ensure that people's basic needs are met and their civil rights are upheld. But we're also working to make sure that everyone gets to experience what brings meaning to life: love, belonging, and joy. These are essential, irreducible needs for all of us. And we can't give people what we don't have. We can't fight for what's not in our hearts.

Again, the key to joy is practicing gratitude. I've interviewed people who have survived serious trauma ranging from the loss of a child to genocide. What I've heard over and over from fifteen years of hearing and holding their stories is this: *When you are grateful for what you have, I know you understand the magnitude of what I have lost.* I've also learned that the more we diminish our own pain, or rank it compared to what others have survived, the less empathic we are to everyone. That when we surrender our own joy to make those in pain feel less alone or to make ourselves feel less guilty or seem more committed, we deplete ourselves of what it takes to feel fully alive and fueled by purpose.

And, sometimes, when we can't acknowledge the pain of others while experiencing our own joy, we close our eyes, insulate ourselves, pretend that there's nothing we can do to make things better, and opt out of helping others. This ability to opt out of suffering and injustice or pretend everything is okay is the core of privilege: *Today I choose not to acknowledge what's happening around me because it's too hard.* The goal is to get to the place where we can think, *I am aware of what's happening, the part I play, and how I can make it better,* and *that doesn't mean I have to deny the joy in my life.*

A wild heart is awake to the pain in the world, but does not diminish its own pain. A wild heart can beat with gratitude and lean in to pure joy without denying the struggle in the world. We hold that tension with the spirit of the wilderness. It's not always easy or comfortable—sometimes we struggle with the weight of the pull—but what makes it possible is a front made of love and a back built of courage.

If we go back to the definition of true belonging, we can see that it's built on a foundation of tensions and paradoxes:

> True belonging is the spiritual practice of believing in and belonging to yourself so deeply that you can share your most authentic self with the world and find sacredness in both being a part of something and standing alone in the wilderness. True belonging doesn't require you to *change* who you are; it requires you to *be* who you are.

And we feel the pull here again in our practices:

People are hard to hate close up. Move in.
Speak truth to bullshit. Be civil.

Hold hands. With strangers.
Strong back. Soft front. Wild heart.

The mark of a wild heart is earned in the wilderness, but there is also a daily practice that I learned from this that is critical to our quest for true belonging. This practice changed how I show up in my life, the way I parent, and the way I lead:

> Stop walking through the world looking for confirmation that you don't belong. You will always find it because you've made that your mission. Stop scouring people's faces for evidence that you're not enough. You will always find it because you've made that your goal. True belonging and self-worth are not goods; we don't negotiate their value with the world. The truth about who we are lives in our hearts. Our call to courage is to protect our wild heart against constant evaluation, especially our own. No one belongs here more than you.

It's not easy to stop looking for confirmation that we don't belong or that we're not enough. At the very least this is a habit for most of us, at worst confirming our inadequacies is a full-time job. When this mandate first emerged from the research, I started working on it, little by little. I would set an intention to stop looking for confirmation that I wasn't smart enough when I walked into a meeting, or that I didn't belong at a parents' meeting at my son's school. I could not believe the power of this practice. My son, Charlie, is in middle school, and my daughter, Ellen, is starting her first year at college. We had a long talk about the validity of this practice, and they both said they could immediately tell a difference in how they were showing up with their friends and in their lives.

Given my personal history and my work, I've always parented with the belief that love and belonging are the ground zero of wholehearted parenting. If they know they are loved and lovable, if they know how to love, and if they know that no matter what, they belong at home, everything else will work out. However, as they got older and peer groups became more important, it was easier than I imagined to slip back into subtly teaching them how to fit in or do whatever it takes to find a crew. My own fear set a default of "Well, what is everyone else wearing?" or "Why weren't you invited to the sleepover—what's wrong?" I have to stay constantly mindful to practice what I believe as a parent and not let fear take over when my kids are hurting.

The importance of belonging at home again became very real to me years ago when I was interviewing a group of middle school students about the differences between fitting in and belonging. I shared these findings in *Daring Greatly*, but it's worth sharing them again here. When I asked a large group of eighth graders to break into small teams and come up with the differences between fitting in and belonging, their answers floored me:

- Belonging is being somewhere where you want to be, and they want you. Fitting in is being somewhere where you want to be, but they don't care one way or the other.
- Belonging is being accepted for you. Fitting in is being accepted for being like everyone else.
- If I get to be me, I belong. If I have to be like you, I fit in.

They nailed the definitions. It doesn't matter where in the country I ask this question, or what type of school I'm visiting—middle and high school students understand how this works. They also talk openly about the heartache of not feeling a sense of belonging at home. That first time I asked the eighth graders to come up with the definitions, one student wrote, "Not belonging at school is really hard. But it's nothing compared to what it feels like when you don't belong at home." When I asked the students what that meant, they used these examples:

- Not living up to your parents' expectations
- Not being as cool or popular as your parents want you to be
- Not being good at the same things your parents were good at
- Your parents being embarrassed because you don't have enough friends or you're not an athlete or a cheerleader
- Your parents not liking who you are and what you like to do
- When your parents don't pay attention to your life

Now, with this new research on true belonging, I know my job is to help my children believe in and belong to themselves. Above all else. Yes, there's always the work of helping them navigate friend situations, and fitting in is a real thing for kids, but our most important task is to protect that tender, wild heart.

We have to resist following them into the wilderness and trying to make it safer and more civilized. Every cell in our body will want to protect them from the hurt that comes with standing alone. But denying our children the opportunity to gain wisdom directly from the trees and dance in the moonlight with the other high lonesome renegades and limping outlaws is about our own fear and comfort. Their hearts need to know the wild too.

As a leader, I want to cultivate a culture of true belonging. I don't want and can't afford fitting in. In my interview with Seattle Seahawks coach Pete Carroll, I was blown away by his answer when I asked him about his time in the wilderness. He said, "Oh, yes. I know that place. I've been fired in the wilderness a couple of times. I'm aware of what's generally accepted from an NFL coach. But sometimes you have to be bold and take chances. And there's a special kind of resilience that comes from the level of scrutiny that happens in the wilderness. I know those experiences left me with a truer belief in myself and a much stronger sense of when I'm not being true to what I think is right."

The resilience that comes from the scrutiny of the wilderness and that "stronger sense of when we're not being true to what we think is right" is the mark of a wild heart. Imagine an organization where a critical mass of people are leading and innovating from a wild heart, rather than following suit, bunkering up, and being safe. We need a wild heart revolution more than ever.

If you want to dig deeper into *Braving the Wilderness* at home or at work, we have parenting and leadership reading guides at brenebrown.com. In my experience, nothing changes until we start putting this work into practice with our families, friends, and colleagues. That's when the wilderness gets real.

Every time I write a book, I'm challenged to live the message. I had to face my own perfectionism when I wrote *The Gifts*. I had to come face-to-face with criticism and courage when I wrote *Daring Greatly*, and I had to challenge all of the stories I make up to protect myself when I wrote *Rising Strong*. Writing this book felt like months of living in the wilderness to me. I kept telling my editor, Ben, that we should just call it *How to Lose Friends and Piss Off Everyone*. If you have strong political opinions, something in here will probably frustrate you. I know there will be lots of disagreement and debate. I hope so. And I hope we'll be fierce and kind with one another.

This is not a call to stop advocating, resisting, or fighting. I will do all three and hope you will too. Our world needs us to show up and stand up for our beliefs. I just hope we're civil and respectful. When we degrade and diminish our humanity, even in response to being degraded and diminished, we break our own wild hearts.

Of all the calls to courage that I've asked readers to answer over the last decade, braving the wilderness is the hardest. It can hurt the most. But, as the quote from Maya Angelou reminds us, it's the only path to liberation.

You are only free when you realize you belong no place—you belong every place—no place at all. The price is high. The reward is great.

I'll leave you with this. There will be times when standing alone feels too hard, too scary, and we'll doubt our ability to make our way through the uncertainty. Someone, somewhere, will say, "Don't do it. You don't have what it takes to survive the wilderness." This is when you reach deep into your wild heart and remind yourself, "I *am* the wilderness."

ACKNOWLEDGMENTS

• • •

THE BBEARG TEAM

I'm deeply grateful to Suzanne Barrall, Cookie Boeker, Ronda Dearing, Olivia Durr, Lauren Emmerson, Barrett Guillen, Sarah Margaret Hamman, Jessica Kent, Charles Kiley, Hannah Kimbrough, Bryan Longoria, Murdoch Mackinnon, Susan Mann, Mashawn Nix, Julia Pollack, Tati Reznick, Deanne Rogers, Ashley Ruiz, Teresa Sample, Sarayu Sankar, Kathryn Schultz, Anne Stoeber, Genia Williams, and Jessica Zuniga.

#bravertogether

THE RANDOM HOUSE TEAM

Big-hearted thanks to my high lonesome editor, Ben Greenberg (the tacos are on me).

And to the Random House team of Gina Centrello, Andy Ward, Theresa Zoro, Maria Braeckel, Lucy Silag, Christine Mykityshyn, Leigh Marchant, Melissa Sanford, Sanyu Dillon, Jessica Bonet, Loren Noveck, and Kelly Chian—thank you for the good work and hard rumbles. I love calling Random House home.

THE WILLIAM MORRIS ENDEAVOR TEAM

To my agent, Jennifer Rudolph Walsh, and the entire team at William Morris Endeavor, especially Tracy Fisher and Eric Zohn, thank you for walking beside me.

THE DESIGNHAUS TEAM

To Wendy Hauser, Mike Hauser, Jason Courtney, Daniel Stewart, Kristen Harrelson, Julie Severns, Kristin Enyart, Annica Anderson, Kyle Kennedy—thank you for the creative badassery.

THE NEWMAN AND NEWMAN.CREW

Thanks to Kelli Newman, Linda Tobar, Kurt Lang, Raul Casares, Boyderick Mays, Van Williams, Mitchell Earley, John Lance, and Tom Francis.

THE HOME TEAM

Love and thanks to Deanne Rogers and David Robinson, Molly May and Chuck Brown, Jacobina Alley, Corky and Jack Crisci, Ashley and Amaya Ruiz; Barrett, Frankie and Gabi Guillen; Jason and Layla Brown, Jen, David, Larkin, and Pierce Alley, Shif Berhanu, Negash Berhanu, Trey

Bourne, Margarita Flores, Sarah Margaret Hamman, Polly Koch, and Eleanor Galtney Sharpe.

WHERE MY WILD HEART TRULY BELONGS

To Steve, Ellen, and Charlie—you are home. *Along with Daisy, Lucy, and Sticky.*

NOTES
• • •

CHAPTER 1

5 I read her poem "Still I Rise": Maya Angelou, *And Still I Rise: A Book of Poems* (New York: Random House, 1978).

5 In an interview with Bill Moyers: Bill Moyers, "A Conversation with Maya Angelou," *Bill Moyers Journal*, original series, Public Broadcasting System, first aired November 21, 1973.

8 the Nicene Creed: en.wikipedia.org/wiki/English_ver sions_of_the_Nicene_Creed.

17 "By the end I was deteriorating": Anne Lamott, Facebook post, July 7, 2015: "On July 7, 1986, 29 years ago, I woke up sick, shamed, hungover, and in deep animal

confusion," facebook.com/AnneLamott/posts/6998541
96810893?match=ZGV0ZXJpb3JhdGluZw%3D%3D.

22 her poem "Our Grandmothers": Maya Angelou, "Our
Grandmothers," in *I Shall Not Be Moved* (New York:
Random House, 1990).

25 Joe Pesci in *Goodfellas*: *Goodfellas*, directed by Martin
Scorsese (United States: Warner Bros., 1990).

28 I got hold of the full transcript: Moyers, "Conversation with Maya Angelou." The interview and full
transcript can be found at billmoyers.com/content/
conversation-maya-angelou/.

CHAPTER 2

31 I defined belonging this way: Brené Brown, *The Gifts
of Imperfection: Letting Go of Who We Think We Should
Be and Embracing Who We Are* (Center City, MN: Ha-
zelden, 2010), p. 26, emphasis added.

34 "Spirituality is recognizing": Brown, *Gifts of Imperfection*, p. 64.

38 "choosing to risk": Charles Feltman, *The Thin Book of
Trust: An Essential Primer for Building Trust at Work*
(Bend, OR: Thin Book Publishing, 2009), p. 7.

38 Seven elements of trust: Brené Brown, *Rising Strong:
The Reckoning. The Rumble. The Revolution* (New York:
Random House, 2015), pp. 199–200.

40 "If you can see your path": The original source of this
quotation is unknown, but it is generally attributed to
Joseph Campbell.

41 "The price is high. The reward is great": Moyers, "Conversation with Maya Angelou."

CHAPTER 3

43 "long, ole, straight bottom part of Kentucky": John Hartford and the John Hartford Stringband, "The Cross-eyed Child," on the album *Good Old Boys* (Nashville: Rounder Records, 1999).

44 "I'm a Man of Constant Sorrow": Roscoe Holcomb, "Man of Constant Sorrow," on the album *An Untamed Sense of Control* (Washington, DC: Smithsonian Folkways Recordings, 2003). This traditional American folk song (original writer/composer unknown) was first published as "The Farewell Song" in a songbook by Dick Burnett around 1913.

44 "I'm Blue, I'm Lonesome": Hank Williams and William S. Monroe (1951), "I'm Blue, I'm Lonesome," recorded by Bill Monroe, on the album *Bill Monroe: The Collection '36–'59* (Location unknown: Ideal Music Group, 2014).

45 the core of that definition of "spirituality": Brown, *Gifts of Imperfection*, p. 64.

46 "As people seek out the social settings they prefer": Bill Bishop, *The Big Sort: Why the Clustering of Like-Minded America Is Tearing Us Apart* (New York: Houghton Mifflin, 2008), p. 14.

47 "As a result, we now live in a giant feedback loop": Ibid., p. 39.

48 I should read Joe Bageant's book: Joe Bageant, *Deer Hunting with Jesus: Dispatches from America's Class War* (New York: Crown, 2007).

49 Veronica Roth's dystopian novel: Veronica Roth, *Divergent*, book 1 of the trilogy known as the Divergent Series (New York: HarperCollins, 2011).

51 At the same time sorting is on the rise, so is loneliness: D. Khullar, "How Social Isolation Is Killing Us," *New York Times*, December 22, 2016, nytimes.com/2016/12/22/upshot/how-social-isolation-is-killing-us.html; C. M. Perissinotto, I. S. Cenzer, and K. E. Covinsky, "Loneliness in Older Persons: A Predictor of Functional Decline and Death," *Archives of Internal Medicine* 172(14), 2012, 1078–83, doi:10.1001/archinternmed.2012.1993; American Association of Retired Persons, "Loneliness Among Older Adults: A National Survey of Adults 45+," September 2010, assets.aarp.org/rgcenter/general/loneliness_2010.pdf.

52 "perceived social isolation": John T. Cacioppo and William Patrick, *Loneliness: Human Nature and the Need for Social Connection* (New York: Norton, 2008).

53 "To grow to adulthood as a social species": John T. Cacioppo, "The Lethality of Loneliness" (TEDxDesMoines transcript, September 9, 2013), singjupost.com/john-cacioppo-on-the-lethality-of-loneliness-full-transcript/, March 7, 2016.

54 "Denying you feel lonely": Cacioppo, quoted in K. Hafner, "Researchers Confront an Epidemic of Loneli-

ness," *New York Times*, September 5, 2016, nytimes
.com/2016/09/06/health/lonliness-aging-health
-effects.html.

54 a "gnawing, chronic disease without redeeming features": R. S. Weiss, *Loneliness: The Experience of Emotional and Social Isolation* (Cambridge, MA: MIT Press, 1973).

55 the brain's self-protection mode often ramps up the stories we tell ourselves: Brown, *Rising Strong*, p. 124.

55 not the quantity of friends but the quality of a few relationships: Susan Pinker, *The Village Effect: How Face-to-Face Contact Can Make Us Healthier and Happier* (New York: Spiegel and Grau, 2014).

55 a meta-analysis of studies on loneliness: J. Holt-Lunstad, M. Baker, T. Harris, D. Stephenson, and T. B. Smith, "Loneliness and Social Isolation as Risk Factors for Mortality: A Meta-Analytic Review," *Perspectives on Psychological Science* 10(2), 2015, 227–37, doi:10.1177/1745691614568352.

60 one of my favorite high lonesome songs: Townes Van Zandt, "If I Needed You," on the album *The Late Great Townes Van Zandt* (New York: Tomato Records, 1972).

CHAPTER 4

63 "I imagine one of the reasons people cling to their hates": James A. Baldwin, "Me and My House," *Harper's Magazine*, November 1955, 54–61.

68 "You will not have my hate": Antoine Leiris, Facebook

post, November 16, 2015 (translated from the French). facebook.com/antoine.leiris/posts/10154457849999 947.

69 "Anger is within each one of you": Kailash Satyarthi, TED talk, March 2015. ted.com/talks/kailash_satyar thi_how_to_make_peace_get_angry?language=en

70 *The price is high. The reward is great*: Bill Moyers, "A Conversation with Maya Angelou," *Bill Moyers Journal*, original series, Public Broadcasting System, first aired November 21, 1973.

72 "Dehumanization is a way of subverting those inhibitions": David L. Smith, *Less than Human: Why We Demean, Enslave, and Exterminate Others* (New York: St. Martin's Press, 2012), p. 264.

72 "the psychological process of demonizing the enemy": Michelle Maiese, "Dehumanization," *Beyond Intractability*, edited by Guy Burgess and Heidi Burgess, Conflict Information Consortium, University of Colorado, Boulder, July 2003, beyondintractability.org/essay/dehumanization.

72 "Once the parties have framed the conflict": Ibid.

78 Joe Paterno's protection of Jerry Sandusky: G. Wojciechowski, "Paterno Empowered a Predator," ESPN, July 12, 2012, espn.com/college-football/story/_/id/8160430/college-football-joe-paterno-enabled-jerry-sandusky-lying-remaining-silent.

79 my friend and colleague Dr. Michelle Buck: My interview with Michelle Buck took place on June 20, 2017. You can read more about Dr. Buck and her re-

search at kellogg.northwestern.edu/faculty/directory/buck_michelle_1.aspx#biography.

83 an interview that I did with Viola Davis: My interview with Viola Davis took place on May 21, 2017.

83 *The Help*: *The Help*, directed by Tate Taylor (United States: DreamWorks Pictures, Reliance Entertainment, Participant Media, Image Nation, 1492 Pictures, & Harbinger Pictures, 2011).

83 *How to Get Away with Murder*: *How to Get Away with Murder*, produced by Shonda Rhimes et al. (Los Angeles, CA: ShondaLand, NoWalk Entertainment, and ABC Studios, 2014–2017).

83 *Fences*: *Fences*, directed by Denzel Washington (United States: Bron Creative, Macro Media, & Scott Rudin Productions, 2016).

83 she was listed by *Time* magazine: N. Gibbs, "The 100 Most Influential People in the World," *Time*, April 20, 2017, time.com/4745798/time-100-2017-full-list/.

CHAPTER 5

89 "Someone who lies and someone who tells the truth": Harry G. Frankfurt, *On Bullshit* (Princeton, NJ: Princeton University Press, 2005), p. 60.

92 "Every nation, in every region": George W. Bush, "President Bush Addresses the Nation," *Washington Post*, September 20, 2001, washingtonpost.com/wp-srv/nation/specials/attacked/transcripts/bushaddress_092001.html.

92 "If you're not with me": *Star Wars: Episode III—*

Revenge of the Sith, directed by George Lucas (United States: Lucasfilm Ltd., 2005).

93 "We must always take sides": Elie Wiesel, Nobel Prize acceptance speech, December 10, 1986. nobelprize.org/nobel_prizes/peace/laureates/1986/wiesel-acceptance_en.html.

94 Bullshit Asymmetry Principle: Tweet by Alberto Brandolini, January 10, 2013. twitter.com/ziobrando/status/289635060758507521?lang=en. (The original tweet used "asimmetry" but the correct spelling has come into common usage.)

95 "Civility is claiming and caring for one's identity": Tomas Spath and Cassandra Dahnke, "What Is Civility?" (n.d.), instituteforcivility.org/who-we-are/what-is-civility/.

96 *Some Girls* by the Rolling Stones: Mick Jagger & Keith Richards, *Some Girls*, recorded by The Rolling Stones (London: Rolling Stones Records, 1978).

104 Leo McGarry: *The West Wing*, produced by Aaron Sorkin et al. (Burbank, CA: John Wells Productions & Warner Bros. Television, 1999–2006).

105 like Meg Ryan in *French Kiss*: *French Kiss*, directed by Lawrence Kasdan (United States & United Kingdom: 20th Century Fox, 1995).

107 "Incivility can fracture a team": C. Porath, "How Rudeness Stops People from Working Together," *Harvard Business Review*, January 20, 2017, hbr.org/2017/01/how-rudeness-stops-people-from-working-together.

108 NFL coach Pete Carroll of the Seattle Seahawks: My interview with Pete Carroll took place on May 10, 2017.

115 "Only the paradox comes anywhere near": C. G. Jung, "Psychology and Alchemy" (1953), in H. Read, M. Fordham, and G. Adler (eds.) and R.F.C. Hull (trans.), *C. G. Jung: The Collected Works*, 2nd ed., vol. 4 (Princeton, NJ: Princeton University Press, 1969), p. 19.

CHAPTER 6

118 "I love mankind . . . it's *people* I can't stand!": gocomics.com/peanuts/1959/11/12/.

118 Pema Chödrön's "Lousy World" teaching: youtube.com/watch?v=buTrsK_ZkvA.

121 a tweet by TED owner and curator Chris Anderson: July 24, 2013, twitter.com/TEDchris/status/360066989420584960.

121 Australian fans of the Liverpool Football Club: "95,000 Liverpool Fans," July 24, 2013, youtube.com/watch?v=F_PydJHicUk.

123 when he sang our collective favorite: D. Linde, "Callin' Baton Rouge" (1978), recorded by Garth Brooks on the CD *In Pieces* (Hollywood, CA: Liberty Records, 1994).

124 we attended opening night: *Harry Potter and the Half-Blood Prince*, directed by David Yates. (United Kingdom & United States: Heyday Films, 2009).

124 what Joseph Campbell called the Hero's Journey: Joseph Campbell and Bill Moyers, *The Power of Myth* (New York: Anchor Books, 1991).

130 the French sociologist Émile Durkheim: Émile Durkheim, *The Elementary Forms of the Religious Life* (1912), translated by J. W. Swain (1915), CreateSpace Independent Publishing Platform, 2016.

130 experiences of *collective assembly*: S. Gabriel, J. Valenti, K. Naragon-Gainey, and A. F. Young, "The Psychological Importance of Collective Assembly: Development and Validation of the Tendency for Effervescent Assembly Measure (TEAM)," *Psychological Assessment* 2017, doi:10.1037/pas0000434.

130 "a sense of meaning, increased positive affect": Ibid.

130 "It is consistent with the idea that collective assembly": Ibid.

132 "Only holiness will call people": John O'Donohue, "Before the Dawn I Begot You: Reflections on Priestly Identity." *The Furrow*, 57:9 (September 2006), p. 471.

132 "How Great Thou Art": Carl Gustav Boberg, "How Great Thou Art," Stuart K. Hine, Trans. Christian hymn, 1885.

132 "Music, uniquely among the arts": Oliver Sacks, *Musicophilia: Tales of Music and the Brain*, revised and expanded edition (New York: Random House, 2007), p. 329.

134 "When we arrived at the cemetery" and following quotes: Sheryl Sandberg and Adam Grant, *Option B: Facing Adversity, Building Resilience, and Finding Joy* (New York: Alfred A. Knopf, 2017), pp. 6, 12, 13.

135 "If you don't have anything nice to say, come sit next to

me": This quotation, in various forms, is generally attributed to Alice Roosevelt Longworth; see e.g. quote investigator.com/category/alice-roosevelt-longworth/.

140 "In a short evolutionary time, we have changed": Susan Pinker, *The Village Effect: How Face-to-Face Contact Can Make Us Healthier and Happier* (New York: Spiegel and Grau, 2014), p. 180.

141 "I call this building your village": Pinker, quoted in C. Itkowitz, "Prioritizing These Three Things Will Improve Your Life—And Maybe Even Save It," *Washington Post*, April 28, 2017, washingtonpost.com/news/inspired-life/wp/2017/04/28/prioritizing-these-three-things-will-improve-your-life-and-maybe-even-save-it/?utm_term=.07f8037a95da.

141 "Research shows that playing cards": Pinker, *Village Effect*, p. 6.

142 We had an entire dance and lip-sync routine: Paul McCartney and Linda McCartney, "Band on the Run," recorded by Paul McCartney and Wings, on the album *Band on the Run* (London, UK: Apple Records, 1974).

CHAPTER 7

147 "All too often our so-called strength comes from fear, not love": Joan Halifax, *Being with Dying: Cultivating Compassion and Fearlessness in the Presence of Death* (Boston: Shambhala Publications, Inc., 2008), p. 17.

150 "I belong to myself. I am very proud of that": Bill

Moyers, "A Conversation with Maya Angelou," *Bill Moyers Journal*, original series, Public Broadcasting System, first aired November 21, 1973.

150 A powerful example of a strong back: Jen Hatmaker, "Hi, everyone. A couple of quick thoughts on all these tender things," Facebook post, October 31, 2016, facebook.com/jenhatmaker/posts/1083375421761452.

155 *"the price is high"*: Moyers, "Conversation with Maya Angelou."

155 "The paradox is one of our most valuable spiritual possessions": Jung, *Psychology and Alchemy (Collected Works of C. G. Jung Vol. 12)*, 2nd ed. (Princeton, NJ: Princeton University Press, 1980), p. 15.

159 When I asked a large group: Brené Brown, *Daring Greatly: How the Courage to Be Vulnerable Transforms the Way We Live, Love, Parent, and Lead* (New York: Gotham Books, 2012).

161 "Oh, yes. I know that place": Author interview with Pete Carroll on May 10, 2017.

163 "You are only free when you realize you belong no place": Moyers, "Conversation with Maya Angelou."

INDEX

• • •

. . .

BRENÉ BROWN, PhD, LMSW, is a research professor at the University of Houston, where she holds the Huffington Foundation–Brené Brown Endowed Chair at the Graduate College of Social Work. She has spent the past two decades studying courage, vulnerability, shame, and empathy and is the author of five #1 *New York Times* bestsellers: *Dare to Lead, Braving the Wilderness, Rising Strong, Daring Greatly,* and *The Gifts of Imperfection.* Her TED talk—"The Power of Vulnerability"—is one of the top five most-viewed TED talks in the world with more than thirty-five million views. Brown lives in Houston, Texas, with her husband, Steve, and their children, Ellen and Charlie.

brenebrown.com
Facebook.com/brenebrown
Twitter: @BreneBrown
Instagram: @BreneBrown

By #1 *New York Times* bestselling author

BRENÉ BROWN

Sign up for Brené's newsletter at
BreneBrown.com.